EATEN BY THE TIGER

SURRENDERING TO AN EMPOWERED LIFE

EMILE A. ALLEN, M.D.

(SURGEON AND PATIENT)

INSPIRE™
ON PURPOSE
Changing Lives With Words

Eaten By The Tiger *by Emile Allen, is a very unusual book. It tells a doctor's story of his catastrophic injury from both sides of the couch, as a doctor and a patient. Dr. Allen writes clearly and frankly, and does not hold back on his most intimate emotions. He describes the terrible accident, his virtual collapse, and the long road back to a better and more meaningful life in a manner that holds the reader's interest from beginning to end. The book is recommended to everybody who has met horrendous circumstances in life (isn't that just about everyone?) and would like help in finding his or her road to recovery and a better life.*

Alma H. Bond, Ph.D.
Author of *Jackie O: On the Couch* and 20 other books

There are some books that move you to tears and some that can help you conquer your fears. In offering us his own story of turmoil and triumphs over life's challenges, Dr. Emile Allen shows us why God spared his life — so he could write Eaten By The Tiger.

Steve Alten
New York Times best-selling author

What an amazing book. It is rare to have a doctor get back in touch with his sensitive side and find that there is more to life than work and status. The spirit and bravery of Dr. Allen are astonishing. Eaten By The Tiger fuels the minds of the reader to reflect on their own life, have gratitude, and let go of disempowering beliefs.

Ninon de Vere De Rosa
President of NinonSpeaks

Eaten By The Tiger *is a truly inspirational story of transformation and growth. Easy to read, hard to put down, and the message stays with you continuously reminding you what's important in life. How Dr. Allen has managed his life changing experience and what he has become will touch all reader's heart, giving us the opportunity to reflect our own life purpose! Highly Recommended Reading! Dr. Allen, Thank you for sharing your story!*

Susan
Pacific Bell/AT&T, Los Angeles

I was riveted to Dr. Emile Allen's book, Eaten by a Tiger. *The spirit he exuded through overcoming adversity to finding a new life purpose was not only refreshing, but inspirational. Thank you for this creative and encouraging work.*

Patricia Kirby
Managing Editor of *Home Care for You*

Excellent read. As a practicing veterinarian attempting to heal the animals in my care, I find Allen's story compelling, inspirational and especially reassuring. His near-death experience and second chance at life will inspire all who face such sudden life-changing crises. He will encourage you to live each day fully, use what you have, forget what you don't and continue using your gifts to help all those in need.

Dan Simpson, DVM

I always have been fascinated by philanthropists who thrive and triumph over their hurdles, whatever they are. The resilience and heroism of Dr. Allen are astonishing. The readers will find in his book many valuable life-lessons endowed with wisdom that can help them flourish. The inspiring story of Dr. Allen has the capacity to heal people by planting empowering seeds in the minds of readers from all walks of life.

Patricia Turnier, Editress-in-Chief
Mega Diversities Web Magazine

What a compelling and inspirational story! Dr. Allen's courage in sharing his struggles of survival inspires all of us to give life a second chance, no matter what has happened.

Rick Rader, M.D.
Editor in Chief Exceptional Parent Magazine

It's often said that you need to walk in someone's shoes to understand their experience. This certainly is true in the book Eaten By The Tiger *by Dr. Emile Allen, where he shares his life-changing experience of being a successful surgeon until tragedy struck. In an actual flash, his life was forever changed. Dr. Allen's vivid description draws the reader into the operating room and through the painstakingly slow motion of the direction of his life. His honesty about his travels through demoralizing depression and despair offers hope to others who may struggle with their own life challenges.* Eaten By The Tiger *is a fascinating read for those who have an interest in things medical as well as for those who enjoy a good mystery, one that beautifully describes one man's search for his identity.*

Elaine Fantle Shimberg
Author of *Blending Families* and 25 other books

Thank you so much for the opportunity to preview Dr. Allen's book. The message is outstanding and written in such a manner that it is understandable to a lay-person. Eaten By The Tiger *gives the reader hope on which they can build.*

Kathleen Foster
Foster Folly News, **Washington County**

Many of us experience tragedy in our lives. A real test of character is how we deal with it. Eaten By The Tiger *by Dr. Allen is a very intimate look at how a man with courage and fortitude dealt struggled with devastating change. His story should inspire many others, especially those in healthcare who can relate so closely to the risks and challenges he faced.*

Marilyn Edmunds, PhD, NP
Editor in Chief of *The Journal for Nurse Practitioners*

As a professional writer for over 20 years, I found this book to be captivating and evocative. Vivid descriptions pulled me into... each story and elicited a visceral and emotional response that not many writers can accomplish...found myself laughing, crying and being shocked by your real life stories...not only engaged my imagination but also demonstrated how to live an empowered life. Thank you, Dr. Allen, for sharing your life with us. Your courage is an inspiration to all of us.

Jeanette Grace
Editor and Writer

Wow! I'm an editor and read books everyday for a living. I couldn't put this book down. The stories are evocative and made me feel like I was right there talking to Dr. Allen. He is a writer and it's obvious he found his true passion.

Donna Kennedy
English Professor and Professional Editor

In clear and simple language, this book describes the process of letting go of the emotional and physical baggage in your life... poignant stories illustrate how to transform yourself into a better you. This is one of the most meaningful books I have ever read, and I highly recommend it as a must have book for your library.

Sid Vaidya, Former VP of IBM
Founder/Chairman, The Diamonds of Diversity

The stories are magnetic, gripping. They pulled me through the book every step of the way.

Sherry Skidmore, Ph.D.
Professor of Forensic Psychology

Since I have recently lost my son, I resonated deeply with Dr. Emile's life stories and insights. My son's passing has left a chasm in my heart and soul so wide and deep, that words can't describe...this book enhanced my faith and will to move forward but not forget the love and joy my son gave...captivating read with extraordinary stories from his life.

Pompey Stafford
Investment Advisor

The weaved stories in the book explore in a realistic and refreshing way how difficult is to let go of the old and face the new, and become the new beings life challenges us to embody when presenting as with adversity. In Eaten By The Tiger, Dr. Emile Allen *shows how the strongest struggles can become the fire that consumes the false in our lives, and let the true remain and flourish. Vivid and encouraging!*

Ira Guevara
Editora El Paracaidista

Inspire On Purpose Publishing

909 Lake Carolyn Parkway, Suite 300

Irving, Texas 75039

(888) 403-2727

Website: http://inspireonpurpose.com

Printed in the United States of America

Library of Congress Control Number: 2012956492

Softcover Print Edition:

ISBN 10: 0989800849

ISBN 13: 978-0-9898008-4-6

*Disclaimer: The names of the patients, families, and some healthcare providers described in this book have been changed for reasons of privacy.

To book Emile for your next speaking event, or for media inquiries, please contact author@EmileAllenMD.com

DEDICATION

I dedicate this book to my loving mother, Betty, and my best friend and father, Browning Allen, who dedicated their lives to those struggling with life's challenges.

Table of Contents

FOREWORD

Eaten By The Tiger is an odyssey about a surgeon's discovery that the whole is greater than the sum of its parts. Emile's magnetic stories pull us through his journey from a life shattered to a life of enlightenment after being eaten by the tiger.

Every person's journey is different and unique. Many of us come to the end of our life and never make the chance, take the chance, or have the chance to put the pieces together. In the end, the question we have is, "Is that all there is in life? Is that it?" All we have left are random, disconnected pieces representing the residue of unresolved pain in our lives. *Eaten By The Tiger* shows us how to process and connect those pieces.

Emile and I first met about four months after his accident. At that time, he was heavily medicated to treat his multiple injuries. Early on, Emile showed three strong qualities: courage, competence, and compassion. These qualities, along with his medical knowledge and technical tools, helped him to persevere and overcome the obstacles he encountered on his path.

Emile is a healer. He is a son, a brother, and an uncle. He is a scientist, a student, and a surgeon. He is a friend, an acquaintance, and a neighbor. Then, he was injured and struggled to find his identity. Like many of my patients, he had difficulty while transitioning from a planned life to a life emanating from the unknown.

In a compartmented world charading as *united*, *merged*, and *managed*, becoming an enlightened person is a challenge. So much of our existence is fragmented to the point where it is hard to find any kind of unity. Against all odds, Emile succeeded in this.

Seldom do we connect with a person who actually tells us: here's my journey, here are my pieces, here's how I am putting them together, and this is where I am in my journey now. Emile provides us with this rare and profound gift.

Emile centers the focus of each story around influential people in his life: Mom, Dad, brother, friends, mentors, doctors, and patients. All served as guides and companions to him on his quest.

Eaten By The Tiger describes and moves us through Emile's many separate roles from an injured surgeon to a healing healer. Emile's words paint graphic stories about his personal journey as he blends his experiences into wholeness. Although he no longer uses his surgeon's scalpel, Emile heals differently now through his book and inspirational speaking.

So many aspects of physical and mental healthcare are based on treating a symptom here and a symptom there, but not on helping a person put their life back together. Emile's unique life story provides us with the missing component to assisting individuals in truly reconstructing their entire lives. Not only will this book be an inspiration to anyone who reads it, but I believe it should be required reading for all clinical psychologists, mental health therapists, and physicians, regardless of their specialty.

I have seen Emile when he was at rock bottom. I have seen him climb to victory when most others would have given up. I am so honored to have had the opportunity to be his doctor and his friend. This book will touch your heart and bring you to a deeper understanding of yourself and others.

Sherry Skidmore, Ph.D.

Dr. Skidmore is a groundbreaking forensic psychologist and Professor of Clinical and Forensic Psychology at California School of Professional Psychology in Los Angeles, California. She currently resides in Riverside, California.

ACKNOWLEDGMENTS

To all of the people who have come into my life, you are a gift. I am appreciative and grateful for each of you.

Even though you are no longer with us, Mom and Dad, thank you for raising me to be the man I am today. I am truly blessed to have had you as my parents. To my two loving brothers, Melvin and Browning, and to my sister-in-law, Jennifer and my niece, Natalie, I thank you for always being supportive during life's weakest moments. To my two sisters, Julie and Marie, and my two nephews, Matthew and Michael, may you be granted the many gifts life has to offer.

To my adopted sister, Sabrina, I am grateful for your sympathetic ear and encouragement. Robyn Coward, I am grateful for your friendship and support during the passing of my mother. You always kept me on the right path by reminding me that time heals wounds.

Thank you, Ernestine Johnson, for stepping up to be my adopted mother after I became an orphan at age 49. You know I love you. For all the funny stories you told, and for hanging out with me over all these years, I thank you, Don Atkins. The Colorado Rocky Mountains will never be the same.

Thank you, Harry Wilkins III, M.D., for being my best friend for 30 years. Northwestern University Medical School taught us well. We both received some amazing gifts in our lives, whether we asked for them or not. May the spirits in the cadaver room live on. To Tony Wilkins, Harry's brother, I am grateful you pushed me beyond my limits and made me do what seemed to be the impossible. Bruce Grizer, NP (Nurse Practitioner), you were my wing buddy for years in delightful and wicked ways. You have been a friend to so many people, and I feel very lucky to be one of them.

I thank you, Arthur Kowell, M.D., Ph.D., for your adeptness. You relentlessly pursued the diagnosis and treatment of the true causes of my conditions when other doctors were unable to do so. For your expertise in pharmacology and your ability to balance my medications, you have my eternal gratitude, Robert "Rocky" Gerner, M.D. You are my angel, Sherry Skidmore, Ph.D. You listened to me and sought to understand the daily struggles I faced during my recuperation. Thank you for putting me on the path to enlightenment.

To all of my urology resident classmates: Greg Lund, Andre Godet, Jay Sandlow, Richard Crusinberry, Jamie McCoy, Eugene Kwon, Ken Ryan, Steve Wahle, Brad Willoughby, Steve Reznicek, Chris Kubat, Jeff Miller, Brad Qualey, and Greg Thompson, we survived the *feeding frenzy* and let it roll off 'like water off a duck's back'. You will all be my fraternal brothers for life.

To all of my professors at the University of Iowa, I appreciate your dedication to higher science and to the development of state-of-the-art medical standards. Richard "Dick" Williams, M.D., you were my professor and close friend. I miss you and thank you for treating all of us residents as family. I know you are happily looking down on us.

William Baker, M.D., this earth is a better place to live for so many people because of you. I miss your presence. Your ultimate sacrifice to save a life at the expense of your own will never be forgotten. You are my hero.

To Janice Brown, Esq., thank you for 20 years of dedicated friendship, patience, and guidance. You were there when the chips were down. I am grateful you kicked me in the ass when I was playing the victim. Russell Foster, I appreciate your life coaching skills and ability to bring out the best in people. Grace Eckert, thank you for your expertise in editing this book and for bringing my vision to life.

INTRODUCTION

Is life getting you down? Are you struggling and frustrated? Do you feel as though nothing fulfills you and the grass is always greener on the other side of the fence? I certainly have.

In 1998, my life took an unexpected turn. I barely escaped electrocution while saving a patient's life. On the other side of my near-death experience, I heard a voice clearly say, *"I'm not ready for you yet. You have more work to do."*

I had no idea that this pivotal moment would be the beginning of my transformative journey of self-discovery. A path that provided answers to the questions most people spend an entire lifetime asking, "Is that it? Is that what life is all about?"

Many never fulfill their dreams, allowing opportunities to pass them by, paralyzed by fear of the unknown.

I call this fear 'The Tiger.' I learned to face 'The Tiger' head-on and embrace it, which empowered me to reach levels of awareness I never knew existed.

In *Eaten By The Tiger*, I share my struggles and the path I took to resolve them. This collection of stories and insights is gleaned from decades of life experiences that helped me to move through the paralysis of emotional and physical loss.

Travel this magnetic journey with me as I show you the path to accept and overcome life's challenges, whether they are emotional, physical, or financial. *Eaten By The Tiger* provides you with the key that opens the door to a more empowered life.

PART I

AWARENESS

*I'm not ready for you yet.
You have more work to do.*

Chapter 1

Awareness: In a Split Second

It was a cold, snowy day on February 26, 1998, as I drove my car down the winding two-lane rural Pennsylvania mountain road from my home to the hospital. The snowflakes were coming down heavily, but it didn't matter. I drove a 4x4 Jeep Grand Cherokee, so I felt quite comfortable driving to work in adverse weather conditions as I had done many times before. Since I performed thousands of operations throughout my career, this was a routine day just like any other.

I arrived at the hospital and headed up to 3 West to make rounds on my patients before going to the operating room. It was going to be a long day. I had a three-hour nephrectomy (removal of the kidney for presumed kidney cancer) and a two-hour radical prostatectomy (removal of the prostate for prostate cancer). I walked from room to room to see my surgery patients from previous days. After writing chart notes and orders for the nurses to continue patient care, I walked down the hallway to the preoperative suite to see my first surgery patient, the three-hour nephrectomy.

Mrs. Davis was a 75-year-old woman I'd seen a few weeks prior. Her chief complaint was chronic left abdominal and back pain. Physical examination and extensive lab reports, including a CAT scan, revealed a large mass in her left kidney. The mass appeared to be renal cancer with no signs that the disease had spread to other organs.

She had multiple medical conditions, including high blood pressure, diabetes, and obesity. Her abdomen was riddled with multiple incisional scars from previous abdominal surgeries for recurrent bowel obstructions and the removal of her gallbladder. I knew this would be a challenging case due to the intra-abdominal scar tissue. The nurses already checked her into the preoperative suite and prepared her for the surgery, which would begin in the next 45 minutes.

When I opened the door of Mrs. Davis' room, her husband and daughter were holding her hand, hugging and kissing her while wishing her the best of luck, praying God would be with her during her operation.

Mrs. Davis jokingly said, "Hi, Dr. Allen. Are you ready to work on this tired old body today?"

I smiled and replied, "Yes, I'm ready. Mrs. Davis, you always make things challenging for your doctors, don't you? This will be your fifth operation."

She laughed. "My husband says I'm a challenge, too, but he doesn't use such nice words."

I reminded Mrs. Davis and her family of the procedure my O.R. team and I would be performing on her that day. Assuring them everything would be fine, I also described what she should expect postoperatively. Despite the individual challenges of this case, the operation itself was a fairly common one for urologists to perform. I expected to discharge her from the hospital in three to four days, if all went as planned.

Mrs. Davis grabbed my hand and said to me, "Dr. Allen, you're my life saver."

When she released her grasp, there was a roll of Life Savers candy in my palm. She was quite the character and one of my favorite patients.

Over the previous weeks, we developed a relationship of mutual respect and trust. I did my best to treat all of my patients as if they were family. My operating room team and hospital staff also knew to adhere to this high standard.

The circulating nurse wheeled Mrs. Davis into the operating room. The O.R. team then placed her on the operating room table and prepared her for surgery. While the anesthesiologist was putting her to sleep, I was in the scrub room following my normal routine of scrubbing my hands and arms to the elbows. As I stood at the scrub sink next to my colleagues who would be helping me with the operation, we talked about what we'd done over the weekend and how our families were doing.

Subsequently, we walked into the operating room, being careful not to contaminate ourselves. The nurse handed each of us a sterile towel to dry our hands. With hands raised in the air, as if we were praying, the surgical nurse placed sterile gowns on us. Once we put our sterile hands through the sleeves, the gowns were tied at the neck and back; then double pairs of sterile gloves were placed on each hand.

By the time we were dressed, Mrs. Davis was completely under anesthesia. The O.R. nurses already prepped and draped her abdomen, leaving the area of the left upper abdomen exposed. This was the area where I would make my incision.

The circulating nurse was responsible for placing the electrocautery grounding pad on the patient's leg and connecting it to the electrocautery unit, an electrical scalpel used by every surgeon. The electrical scalpel looks like a pencil with a toggle switch that can be pushed to either cut tissue or cauterize blood vessels to control bleeding.

I used this machine thousands of times throughout my career. It is a vital piece of equipment used to decrease blood loss and improve operating time. This allowed me to complete the surgery as quickly as possible and get the patient off the operating room table, thus decreasing the risk of complications.

To gain access to the internal organs, I made my initial 14-inch incision in the left upper quadrant of the abdomen, just a few inches underneath the left rib cage. Immediately, I encountered a large amount of scar tissue from her previous surgeries for bowel obstructions. Meticulously, I dissected away the scar tissue and the sheath of tissue covering the bowel. I was able to move the left colon in order to gain access to the area of the left kidney. All was going well.

I held the bowel in my left hand, freeing it from the adjacent organs by using the electrical scalpel in my right hand. Suddenly, in a split second, a large popping sound and an arc of electricity shot out of the electrical scalpel. The arc blew through the patient's bowel and into my left finger, coursed up my arm— and as I found out the next day—through my heart and brain, and made its final exit out my right ankle. In this split second, the electrical force threw me back approximately six to eight feet, and I collapsed onto the operating room floor.

Everyone in the room was stunned. They couldn't believe what just happened. When I first hit the floor, I was screaming in pain and holding my hand as I saw blood quickly fill up my surgical glove. The nonstop burning pain was excruciating and unlike any I experienced before. Imagine the pain you would feel if your hand were severed at the wrist without anesthesia. That was the pain I was feeling radiate up my arm and through my shoulder. I kept screaming, begging someone to stop the pain.

One of the staff nurses immediately crouched beside me, took the gloves off, and poured sterile saline solution over my hand to see the extent of the wound. It was a small burn about the size of a pinhead on my middle finger. How could such a small wound cause so much damage? An artery was pumping bright red blood from the first joint of my finger. The nurse placed pressure on it while I continued to scream in pain.

Quickly, I felt cold, clammy, and weak. I rapidly went into shock. As they were losing me, I had a seizure on the cold, sterile operating room floor.

My O.R. team frantically ran around the room, shouting orders, "Call a CODE! Get the crash cart!"

Although I could still see a blur of my colleagues, I could no longer hear the sounds of everyone trying to save my life. The room became quiet. Everything went dark. The physical suffering vanished, and I felt at peace.

I don't know how long I was out, perhaps seconds or minutes, but during that time in the darkness, I heard a voice say:

"I'm not ready for you yet. You have more work to do."

This voice came from an amorphous figure, an ill-defined shape of a person's face that came out of the shadows and entered my right upper visual field. I couldn't tell if the voice was a man or a woman. I just heard the voice. Again, it said:

"I'm not ready for you yet. You have more work to do."

I woke up suddenly to the unbearable pain. This time

it was even more intense than before. Once again, I was screaming at the top of my lungs, "Make it stop! Make it stop! Please make it stop! Do whatever you have to do, just stop the pain."

I pleaded with the anesthesiologist, "Please, please do a nerve block on my hand! Please stop the pain! Just block the nerve! Block the nerve! Block the nerve!"

The anesthesiologist complied and anesthetized the major nerve to my hand. Within a few minutes, the pain started to subside. While it was not entirely gone, the nerve block certainly diminished the pain to a tolerable level.

The staff placed me on a gurney and wheeled me out of the operating room to the recovery room down the hallway. Here, they could hook me up to a cardiac monitor to track my vital signs and neurological status. I was drenched in sweat, cold and shivering. Feeling quite lethargic and dopey, I kept nodding off without realizing it.

The brain fog left me disoriented to the point that I wasn't sure where I was or who was around me. Various doctors, including a neurologist and a cardiologist, examined me and said I was going to be fine. In the opinion of these doctors, I was properly oriented enough to leave the hospital. Despite that fact, deep inside I knew something was not right. I just felt off.

After about an hour, I started to feel a little bit better when I remembered the surgery and asked, "Oh my God, what happened to Mrs. Davis? Is she okay?"

"Don't worry," the recovery room nurse said. "Dr. Sanders took over your case. He repaired the electrical injury to the bowel and is ready to remove her kidney."

That really shook me awake. I knew Dr. Sanders did not know how to perform the type of kidney surgery I had planned. He would need my guidance to ensure the cancer operation would be successful for Mrs. Davis' particular disease.

I realized that I must return to the operating room as soon as possible to help him. I set my recent trauma aside, and my brain went into autopilot mode. As I climbed off the gurney, I pulled off the cardiac monitor leads, removed the oxygen cannula, and took out my IV.

The recovery room nurse protested, "Dr. Allen, what are you doing? You can't leave here yet. You are not ready. You need to be monitored awhile longer."

I kept moving. "I have to get back to the operating room. Dr. Sanders doesn't know what my patient needs. It is not a simple removal of the kidney."

Although I was not planning to operate with a numb hand, I simply had to do what was best for my patient if at all possible.

Somehow, I scrubbed into the operation again and stood by Dr. Sanders while I talked him through the detailed surgical process. The operation was successful, and Mrs. Davis recovered remarkably well. After the surgery, when the adrenaline rush faded, I was so exhausted that I wanted to fall asleep.

I had another surgery scheduled for that day, but the O.R. staff cancelled the case and suggested I go home to rest. Even though I still did not feel *right*, I drove the 15 minutes home alone in my Jeep in a snowstorm over winding rural roads.

After I got home at about noon, my fatigue and confusion worsened. I kept asking myself, 'What did they give me while I was in the hospital? Did they give me a narcotic or some drug that is making me lethargic?'

I found out later that they hadn't. They hadn't given me anything besides the nerve block for my hand injury. Nevertheless, I was so tired that I crawled into bed and slept nonstop from about 1:00 p.m. until 2:00 a.m. the following morning.

I woke up in the middle of the night disoriented, confused, and weak. Something told me to call my parents and tell them what happened. My dad, a semi-retired urologist, still worked as the medical director of a kidney stone center in Pomona, California. My mother was a retired nurse who taught thousands of nursing students throughout her career.

When I called them, my speech was so slurred Mom didn't recognize my voice and kept asking, "Who is this? Hello. Who is this?"

"Mom, it's me. Emile."

"Emile, are you okay?"

"I got electrocuted and almost died today from the electrocautery unit," I drowsily answered.

Mom was absolutely aghast. She screamed for my Dad.

"Browning! Browning! Get on the phone right away! Something happened to Emile!"

Dad barked, "Betty, what's wrong?"

Mom yelled, "Browning, just get on the phone! Emile is hurt."

Once both Mom and Dad were on the phone, I explained what happened from what I could recall and what others had told me.

"We'll be on the next flight to see you," Mom said.

"Okay, I'm tired right now. I'm going to sleep."

Dad barked again in his old Army MASH unit voice, "Emile, you get back to the hospital right now. The doctors should never have sent you home."

As usual, I argued. "No, I'm okay. I'll be fine. Don't worry about me. I'm just tired."

I went back to sleep and woke up at 6:00 a.m., still feeling exhausted. Since there was not another urologist on staff to take over my cases, I felt an obligation to go into the hospital, no matter what. I was still groggy and didn't recall taking a shower, putting on my surgical scrubs, or driving into work. I arrived at the hospital to make rounds on my patients. Apparently, I had made my rounds and even written orders while still on autopilot since I couldn't remember what I'd done.

After I'd left the hospital in a fog, I walked across the street to my office where Julie, my nurse, and Cheryl, my secretary, were happy to see me; however, they obviously didn't think I should be at work. They kept asking me if I was all right. I just wanted people to leave me alone and let me see my patients, but my staff already cancelled most of my appointments, except for three patients they could not reach. When the first patient showed up, I grabbed the chart on the outside of the door and walked into the room to evaluate her situation.

This middle-aged woman had bladder cancer, no doubt caused by her long smoking habit. While I was taking her medical history, I literally fell asleep. At first, she kept asking me if I was all right. Then, she began shaking me. When I wouldn't wake up, she called for help.

"Help! Come quickly! There is something wrong with Dr. Allen!"

Julie ran in the room to witness me slumping down in my chair and leaning against the wall, chart still in hand.

"Oh, my God! Dr. Allen! Dr. Allen! Are you okay?"

She shook me until I woke up. I said, "I'm fine. Nothing's wrong with me. I'm fine."

I couldn't understand what was causing all the fuss. "What's wrong with you? I'm just trying to see my patient, and you keep interrupting me."

Julie ignored me and insisted, "Dr. Allen, we're taking you back to the hospital now! Cheryl! Grab me the blood pressure cuff and thermometer."

"I don't need to go to the hospital," I said. "I just feel tired from yesterday. I'm fine."

They said, "No, Dr. Allen, you need to go to the hospital now!"

I was being stubborn and still didn't want to go. "First, let me call my friend Harry and tell him what's going on," I said.

At the time, Harry was a trauma surgeon in Kansas City. As fellow medical school students, we survived the vigorous training and intense experiences of becoming an M.D. Harry is second to none, and I trusted him with my life.

When I called Harry, he was stern with me. "Emile, I've known you for close to 16 years. You don't sound good. You've got to listen to me. You've had a severe electrical injury with a near-death experience, and they brought you back."

He went on to say, "You need to get into a hospital right away because you could have cardiac and neurological damage. Plus, you've had a severe electrical burn injury to the nerve in your hand. All of this needs to be evaluated immediately. The doctors should never have released you from the hospital yesterday."

After Harry told me this, I said, "Okay, I'll listen to you guys and go to the hospital."

I only agreed to this under the condition that I would be admitted to a larger medical center with more expertise in neurology and electrical injuries. Admission to the hospital seemed to be the lesser of two evils and a better option than listening to the two of them lovingly nag at me.

Cheryl insisted on driving me. Julie decided to stay back to take care of the three patients remaining in the office.

Cheryl put me into the car and drove me to the medical center that had the specialists I needed. Upon arrival, the staff immediately admitted me to the intensive care unit and placed me on neurological checks every two hours.

Although my specialists felt I suffered a mild concussion, a CAT scan and an MRI of the brain did not reveal any obvious damage. Test results indicated a mild injury to my heart. Since my left hand was weak and wouldn't close, the specialists were most concerned about the neurological damage to my hand. My fine motor coordination was disrupted entirely, and I could not hold or pick up objects.

I was in the intensive care unit for a couple of days. Tubes and wires were on every part of my body. Monitors beeped day and night, and I was sure the entire hospital staff came into my room every five minutes. I was kept awake so much that I became severely sleep deprived.

The day I was admitted to the hospital, my mom and dad arrived from California, but I couldn't identify either of them. I only recognized my nurse and my secretary, Julie and Cheryl. I couldn't remember the doctors traversing in and out of my room, so I kept asking for their names. Mom and Dad were concerned, but the doctors told my parents that the concussion seemed mild and should resolve soon.

After a few days, my memory started to come back, and I felt more alert and oriented.

"Mom. Dad," I said. "When did you get here?"

"We've been here for three days," Mom told me.

Tears of happiness flowed down her face, and I think I even saw a drop fall from one of my dad's eyes.

Though my memory improved, I couldn't remember the accident. Hearing the story from others was the only way I was able to reconstruct the accident and the events that followed. By then, I understood what transpired, and I was happy to be alive.

On day four of admission, my doctors transferred me from ICU to a step-down unit on the main floor where they placed me on a regimen of physical therapy and whirlpool baths for my hand. I spent a week in the hospital before leaving with a diagnosis of a mild concussion, left median nerve injury, and mild cardiac muscle damage.

Since my mom was retired, she stayed with me for close to a month. Dad, however, could only stay for about two weeks before returning to work. Mom drove me to and from physical therapy to have treatments on my hand over the ensuing month. Every time I passed the hospital on my way to physical therapy, I felt like the accident had just happened. The emotional pain reminded me of the physical damage I incurred. My lethargy waxed and waned, and I slept frequently throughout the day, unsure whether it was due to the lack of sleep in the ICU or from the electrical injury.

I wore a brace on my arm and hand to prevent the muscles from contracting. In spite of that, over the next three months, the muscles in my left hand and arm atrophied down to nothing but skin overlying bone, tendons, and ligaments.

I also developed reflex sympathetic dystrophy (RSD) of my left arm and hand. A person with this condition experiences the frequent and painful feeling of *pins and needles*, similar to a foot or forearm that has fallen asleep and is just waking up. The skin of my arm and hand was mottled in various shades of red and purple. I also had extreme sensations of hot and cold with profuse sweating for no apparent reason. The physical therapists and doctors continued to be particularly concerned about my arm and hand, wondering what their ultimate function would be.

After a month of treatment from the doctors, I wasn't getting any better, so my parents decided it was best that I live with them in Southern California and see specialists located near their home.

As a result of this decision, I had to close my practice, which was the hardest thing I could possibly do. Some of my closest friends, doctors, and patients sent me beautiful, heartfelt cards and letters, making the ending even more bittersweet. All of my patients depended on me so much, and I would certainly miss them. I was the only urologist for this rural community with a population draw of over 200,000 people. Who would take care of them?

I was now also realizing that my identity, as I had known it, was beginning to fall apart. With this change, I knew I was losing my independence, my job security, and my financial well-being. I felt deep loss and was uncertain of where my life was going. I didn't know if my hand would function again or whether I'd be able to practice surgery. At the same time, I felt embarrassed and was grieving over my loss. I just wanted to get out of there and make the nightmare go away.

Once established in California with my new specialists, my specific physical issues became their focus. The doctors thought my symptoms of lethargy and depression were the result of the post-traumatic stress disorder (PTSD); however, no one paid very much attention to the chronic fatigue I was experiencing. Therefore, in addition to the various medications I was taking for my hand injury, I was also given antianxiety drugs and antidepressants. At this point, I was taking 36 pills a day from nine different prescriptions. It was overwhelming.

Repeatedly, I told my doctors that something else was wrong with me. I felt I was having side effects from the medications. Instead of listening to my complaints and taking me off some of the medications or at least reducing the dosage, they would give me yet another prescription to add to the cocktail of medications I was already taking. This was extremely frustrating to me.

I felt powerless.

Despite the fact that I was working with my medical colleagues, I felt insignificant. They were not respecting my knowledge of my body as a physician or a patient. It was the norm to be rushed out of the office without getting my questions answered. I felt belittled. To ensure treatment costs were covered, I was even fighting with the insurance carriers. My identity was changing, and it was definitely affecting my self-esteem. What was I going to do? My life as a surgeon seemed over.

Due to the constant pain I was experiencing in my arm and hand, my physicians suggested I take narcotics, which I immediately refused. I just couldn't take another pill. Another reason I declined was because I'd seen so many patients over my medical career struggle with addiction to prescription narcotics. Instead, I used biofeedback and meditation, along with various medications, to help control my chronic arm and hand pain, migraine headaches, PTSD, and clinical depression.

Many days I was so weak from my condition and side effects of all of the medications that I could hardly get out of bed. Adjustments in dosages or additional medications were required to counteract the side effects from the nine prescriptions I was already taking. It was a no-win situation! I was in a destructive loop that I could not get out of at the time. As I was losing my sense of self, I felt powerless and hopeless.

About five months after my accident, when I was dealing with this set of circumstances, Mom called the family to dinner. Everyone showed up at the table, except me. Mom came to my room to see if I was sleeping. Instead, I was having a seizure. I was immediately taken to see a new neurologist associated with UCLA Medical Center, Arthur Kowell, M.D.

I underwent an extensive evaluation of my brain with SPEC scans, CAT scans, MRIs, and EEGs. Dr. Kowell discovered what the others didn't. I had sustained a brain injury from the accident that was causing my chronic lethargy and the new onset of seizures. I then progressed to having problems with concentration to the point where I could not read a book or count change.

At age 38, the peak of my surgical career, I was now entirely dependent on my aging parents to take care of me. However, the big hit came when Dr. Kowell told me that I should not drive anymore. He felt my brain injury, seizures, and high doses of various medications made it unsafe for me to operate a vehicle. As hard as it was, I knew he was right.

As a result, I needed to be driven anywhere I wanted or needed to go, such as the grocery store, the mall, the dentist, or the movie theater. If I wanted to go on a date, my parents took me. I felt like I was a 14-year-old all over again. It was exceedingly frustrating. Here I was, an M.D. with 13 years of professional education and seven years in private practice who'd taught medical students and residents, served as an expert witness, and held positions as chairman of urology and vice-chairman of surgery at a prestigious medical center. That split second in the operating room took away the value of all my education and experience.

What a blow! What was I going to do with my life if I did not get better? Life seemed as if it were over. My depression deepened.

Due to my brain injury, my doctors sent me to a clinical psychologist, Sherry Skidmore, Ph.D., for extensive neuropsychological testing to gather baseline information. Results found my IQ dropped over 50 points from a previous baseline level. No wonder I was having trouble functioning in basic daily activities. This *subtle* brain injury was not so subtle after all.

Nowadays, because of the Iraq and Afghanistan wars, the medical community recognizes the condition known as traumatic brain injury (TBI). Back in 1998 when my accident occurred, few experts knew about TBI, let alone how to look for it.

Unfortunately, I was still having many debilitating side effects from the medications I was taking. Sherry referred me to Robert Gerner, M.D., a psychiatrist specializing in pharmacology, who took on the task of managing all of my medications. With some trial and error, he was able to adjust my medications to the point of eliminating 90% of the side effects I'd been experiencing. This dramatically improved my physical and emotional well-being.

While the struggles I encountered were demoralizing and my self-esteem was at rock bottom, I now had hope. After about six months, the right team of doctors was finally in place. They figured out what was actually going on with me, adjusted my medications to decrease side effects, and put me on the path to recovery. Every day I am grateful to Dr. Kowell, Dr. Gerner, and Dr. Skidmore (Sherry) for coming into my life. As a matter of fact, all the doctors and nurses who cared for me from the day of my injury did their best with the information available at the time.

I now had a list of diagnoses that included traumatic brain injury (TBI), post-traumatic stress disorder (PTSD), loss of cognitive function, seizures, debilitating migraine headaches, reflex sympathetic dystrophy (RSD), left hand numbness, difficulties with fine motor coordination, and severe atrophy of my left arm and hand. Life was not looking so great right about then.

I was scared. I was trying to hold onto what little identity I had left as a physician and surgeon, and I didn't know what I was going to do or could do with my life. Would I ever get back to where I was or who I was? With all of this medical knowledge trapped inside me, I kept asking myself, 'What career can I have that still uses my medical background?'

Would the seizures ever stop? How long would this excruciating pain in my arm and hand last, and would their function return to normal? Would I be on medications forever? Would I ever drive or live on my own again? I had many questions but no answers. Only time would tell.

Physicians, friends, and family kept saying that I was depressed and that things would get better. It just takes time. From a medical standpoint, I certainly felt depressed. However, I knew it was more than that. I was grieving. I was mourning a huge list of losses. I lost my freedom and my independence. I lost my career, my status in the community, and my patients. I lost my home, my lifestyle, and my significance as a man. I lost so many things — and all at the same time. I soon realized I was grieving over the loss of my identity, which was manifesting as the signs and symptoms of clinical depression.

That was my first insight. I became aware and knew that I'd lost my identity. Now I needed to figure out what I was going to do about it.

Chapter 2

Awareness: The Descent

As I continued to stay with my parents and receive care from my medical team, the real impact of my loss of identity became much clearer. During this time, the pain from my reflex sympathetic dystrophy (RSD) was increasing. My arm and hand were in such excruciating pain that it felt as though the accident were happening all over again.

To control this pain, I was undergoing hyperbaric oxygen therapy and anesthesia nerve block treatments at the hospital. The nerve block treatments consisted of a six-inch needle injected into my neck and down along the vertebrae into my chest cavity. I received these nerve blocks once a week for close to four months in order to try to break the pain cycle.

One day, after receiving one of these nerve block injections, I developed a severe infection that spread from my neck into my chest cavity. I became extremely ill, requiring extensive antibiotic therapy and pain medications. Once again, I was laid up at home for a week not knowing which way my health would turn.

While I was recovering and reflecting on life's change of events, I heard the same voice as I did while I was lying on the operating floor fighting for my life:

"I'm not ready for you yet. You have more work to do."

This message played repeatedly in my head. What did it mean? I had no idea. What could I possibly contribute when everything was collapsing within me and around me?

After recovering from the infection, I went back to San Diego to visit some of my colleagues, most of whom I hadn't seen in years. The breakdown of my identity continued. As I entered the hospital, the feel and smell reminded me of the good old days. I felt energized. Assuming I was among friends, I shared the details of my accident with them, explaining that I still had seizures because of a brain injury and struggled with nerve damage to my arm and hand. Due to this, I told them my career as a surgeon was over.

As I was telling my story, certain doctors seemed to look at me in a disinterested manner as if they had enough of their own problems and couldn't care less. I felt discounted and judged. While I am sure they didn't mean to be short with me, this was how I felt.

To add insult to injury, one of the doctors even quickly scanned me over and blurted out, "Well, you don't look too bad. You'll be fine. Just give it some time."

I remember saying to myself, 'What a jerk! You have no idea of the pain and suffering I'm going through right now. I'm just trying to make it to the next day.'

As opposed to taking the time to find out what problems or struggles their patients might be experiencing, I realized that many physicians make snap judgments based on appearance alone.

Sometimes, a patient's medical condition is more than just the physical injury. The associated psychological injuries are oftentimes just as significant, if not more. However, physicians rarely consider this during their evaluation and treatment of a patient. A person can be stuck in a continuous circuit of physical and emotional suffering, making it hard to get out of the loop. I learned this firsthand.

These reactions from my medical colleagues seemed hurtful and degrading, especially since they had known me for so many years. I felt demoralized and lost. Even though this wasn't true, I felt as though I'd been kicked out of *The Club* where I'd earned my place and had been a prestigious member. I thought I would be safe with them, no matter what happened. How could they make such a snap diagnosis without examining me or knowing anything about my situation?

They based their judgments solely upon how I looked in their eyes at that particular moment, not on what was truly going on in my life. However, it did not end with my colleagues, all of whom were trained medical professionals. This also occurred when I met friends and people in the general public who had no medical knowledge whatsoever. They, too, made snap judgments about me.

Because I couldn't deal with the judgments I felt I would receive, I withdrew into my shell even more. It got to the point that I didn't want to tell anyone I was a surgeon. Every recounting of my story placed me back at the time of my accident, which reminded me of my deep and painful losses. I was just too fragile emotionally and physically at that point to withstand the stress of these potentially toxic interactions. I saw no light at the end of the tunnel and felt each new listener would trample on my self-esteem.

In addition to these humiliations, I was dealing with a traumatic brain injury (TBI) and seizures, both of which caused memory loss. Given that I had difficulties concentrating and performing simple math skills, I was extremely frustrated. For over three years, going to the store was a significant event because I couldn't count the change. Since this was in the days before debit cards, I would put cash down and hope it was for the right amount. I felt so embarrassed, and I prayed no one would notice.

It also took three years after my injury to get to the point where I could read a book from cover to cover. The first book I was able to read was *Tuesdays with Morrie*, by Mitch Albom. It still sits on my bookshelf as a reminder of how far I have come.

Sherry felt it would be an excellent idea for me to enroll in art classes to get the creative side of my brain working as this would help connect the neurons and repair the injury. After about a year of art classes, I started to view things differently. Rather than seeing a vase as simply a vase, I began to perceive the shadows of the vase. From this viewpoint, I could see the complexity of a scene enriched by the shadows that emerged from the objects. This reflected to me how I was seeing others and myself with more shadow and nuance, giving life a new perspective.

After I'd made enough progress on my math skills and concentration, I applied for jobs; however, that wasn't working out as planned. I still required two to three hours of naps throughout the day because of my disability and side effects of medication, which interfered with a full-time job.

I found it very difficult to find a job in the healthcare field. As a result of my injuries, I could no longer be a surgeon. I just couldn't picture going back to do another three- to six-year residency program all over again. It would be too demanding and demoralizing. I researched medical director positions at pharmaceutical and medical device companies, but I could not get a break. Either they were not looking at that time, or I was too specialized. The longer I was without work, the more difficult it was to explain the lapse. Three, four, five years had gone by. I wasn't lazy. I wanted to work, be productive, and contribute to society; however, what was my niche?

I continued to struggle. I was trudging slowly and painfully, but progressing nonetheless, through the first step of creating a new identity: becoming aware. I was aware of the loss I'd suffered and that my identity had been changed forever; however, I only had the questions, not the answers.

Who is Emile? What is my identity? What am I supposed to do with my life? My journey to seek the
answers was just beginning.

Chapter 3

Awareness: Chosen Destiny

Oftentimes, the influence of others who are significant in our lives can persuade our destiny. As I was contemplating the loss of my identity, I wondered, 'Is the identity I am shedding truly what I'd wanted to become in the first place?'

Perhaps I hadn't become the person I intended or was meant to be. In addition to other influences along my path, I reflected back on my childhood and began to realize some truths about my upbringing. I was awakening to the fact that my career choice, like many, was redirected from my original passion.

In some ways, my life path seemed preordained. From the age of seven, my parents were grooming me to become a surgeon. My father was a urologist in private practice and a professor of urology at the University of Southern California (USC) Medical Center in Los Angeles, California. He would take me on rounds with him at the hospital where I was able to see his excellent bedside manner. He treated his patients like family, a skill I naturally adopted.

I would go to the O.R. and watch him perform surgeries. Here I was, a seven year old in scrubs, sitting on a swivel chair by the anesthesiologist. The doctor let me monitor the patient's vital signs and taught me how the various anesthetics kept patients asleep during surgery. He would also put me on a stool so I could see over the curtain and watch Dad perform his surgeries. Dad taught me how to diagnose various diseases such as kidney stones, urinary tract infections, bowel obstructions, and appendicitis. I also learned the basics of anatomy, physiology, and radiology from him.

My mom did the same thing. As a registered nurse, she taught nursing at Mount San Antonio Community College in Diamond Bar, California, and worked at Pomona Valley Hospital on the orthopedic and labor and delivery floors. She frequently took me to see the newborn babies and even brought me into the pediatric intensive care unit where I saw the newborns in the incubators or on ventilators. I remember the nurses allowing me to hold a two-pound preemie in my hand.

The infant was so tiny and fragile!

These childhood experiences were unusually intense and made a real impression on my young, vulnerable psyche. I felt it was normal to do these things with one's parents and continued to visit the hospital during my adolescent years and through college. However, my true passion was my love for animals.

When I was 12 years old, I had a three-year-old horse named Jobay. He was a beautiful chocolate-brown horse with a black mane and tail. There was a white star on his forehead and huge, soft, dark-brown eyes in which you could lose yourself. Jobay was gentle, and I knew he would never harm me in any way. During our long conversations, he proved to be an excellent listener. He responded to what I said with love and understanding by nodding his head or nuzzling his nose on my face or hands. For being a *good boy*, I would often give him carrots and apples, which were his favorite treats.

He was my best friend and was more like a dog than a horse to me; however, I had to share his affection with the barn cat, Chula, who would get up on the fence by the corral and jump on Jobay's back to go for a ride. Not only did Jobay allow this, but he also encouraged this behavior by walking up to the fence to pick up his small passenger from time to time. Sometimes I would even catch Chula splayed out on Jobay's back taking an afternoon nap. The dogs would also play and sleep with Jobay. He was the heart of our little menagerie. What memories!

The summer following sixth grade, I convinced my mom to buy a six-week-old baby pig to add to the farm. He was a cute little guy that we named Wilbur after the character in *Charlotte's Web*. When we brought him home, he was so scared that he squealed constantly and was afraid to be touched. This was understandable since he'd just been taken away from his mother and eight other littermates, put in a box, and driven 20 minutes to a new environment.

We put Wilbur in a pen in the backyard; however, he was so small and agile that he was able to squeeze out from under the pen fence. Wilbur was running around loose in the yard with the dogs chasing after him. Man, could Wilbur run fast! When my dad drove up, Mom, my brother, and I were also chasing Wilbur trying to catch him. It was a crazy mess. Dad was extremely angry because he specifically said he didn't want any more animals. He jumped out of the car cussing at all of us. Then, Dad said, "Betty, why did you buy that damn pig???"

Mom replied, "Oh, Browning. He's so cute. Besides he'll keep Emile out of trouble and give him a project for the 4-H Club."

Between the dogs and all of us, including one pissed-off father, we finally cornered Wilbur by a woodpile. However, Dad was so mad that he pushed us away yelling, "Get out of the way! Let me get this damn pig!"

When Dad reached down to grab him, surprisingly, Wilbur jumped up like a dog, bit my dad on the leg, and ran away. We were all so shocked — even the dogs were! Dad said, "That SOB bit me!"

We all cracked up in laughter. What a day! We finally caught Wilbur and put him into a smaller pen by the house. Eventually, the dogs became friends with Wilbur, and they all played together. Wilbur even grew on Dad and became part of the family.

A few days later, two friends who played football for Stanford University stopped by the house. One of the guys wasn't paying very much attention to me because I was just a kid, which annoyed me. Obviously, he didn't know much about being around animals since he happened to be wearing white pants, and you don't wear white pants on a farm.

Wilbur was stressed out from moving to a new environment with different food and developed diarrhea. Given that I didn't care much for this guy, I decided to play a trick on him.

"Would you help me move Wilbur from the pen by the house to the barn? He's a little bit too heavy for me to carry on my own," I said.

"Sure. No problem," he said.

"Since pigs can bite, let me tell you how to pick up the pig. You take the back legs, and I'll take the front legs."

He agreed, all the while looking uncertain and even a little scared. In light of the fact that he was a star player, he sucked it up and helped me.

My family knew exactly what I was doing, yet didn't warn the college athlete. When he picked up the pig's back legs, Wilbur squealed and splattered diarrhea all over the star's white pants. The guy was furious! My dad was laughing so hard tears were streaming down his face. I doubled over in laughter to the point where I could barely stand up. Despite Mom scolding me for my mischievous prank, even she broke out in uncontrollable laughter. I then picked up Wilbur by myself and took him down to the other pen. I never did need his help. I just didn't like him.

We also had some baby lambs and a cow at our little farm. One day before going to school when I was 13, I went out to the barn to feed the animals. One of the lambs was gone, so I looked around the yard and found the lamb by herself covered in blood. On the right side of her body was an eight-inch flap of skin that was torn and stripped to the muscle going up about six inches. Apparently, a pack of stray dogs or coyotes visited during the night and attacked the poor little lamb. Luckily, she survived the brutal assault.

I ran up to the house and called my dad to help, but he was on his way to the hospital. Seeing the extent of my distress, he immediately decided to call his office to reschedule his patients and came to the lamb's rescue. I took her into the barn, and Dad arrived with his doctor's bag to provide medical attention.

I held the lamb while Dad cleaned the wound and sutured the muscles and skin back together. Dad told me that since the blood supply was damaged, he wasn't sure the skin flap would survive. He said it was okay if the skin didn't reattach because the wound would heal from the inside out.

Dad said, "Son, this is healing by secondary intention."

I didn't understand how this could happen but was soon to find out.

I took care of the lamb before and after school every day. After about three days, I got up to check on the lamb and found her looking better and running around.

However, like something out of a horror movie, I saw small white things moving underneath the skin flap where the sutures were starting to fall out. I grabbed the lamb, pulled away the skin flap and saw hundreds of white maggots crawling in the wound.

I freaked out and ran up to the house yelling, "Dad! Dad! Something is killing the lamb!"

Dad quickly came down to see what was going on. He calmly examined the wound, smiled and said, "That's okay, Son. The wound actually looks really good."

Dad took out the rest of the sutures and cut away the skin flap that was not going to survive. Then, he took some betadine and washed off the maggots. The maggots cleaned out the wound by eating away the dead tissue, leaving fresh, pink, healthy tissue.

My dad explained to me that physicians used leeches from WWI through the Korean War to clean soldiers' wounds, which allowed the wound to close by secondary intention. These maggots were doing the same thing as the leeches. In a few weeks, the lamb's eight-inch wound healed from the inside out with barely a scar. At age 13, this experience helped me see that I wanted to be a doctor to animals rather than to people. I felt that I'd found my passion.

Although my parents' desire was to groom me to become a physician, I knew I wanted to be a veterinarian. I even went to the University of California, Davis (UC Davis) for undergrad with the intention of applying to veterinary school there. In the 1980s, there were approximately 21 veterinary schools throughout the entire country, a far smaller number than the amount of medical schools at the time. Therefore, it was easier to get into medical school than it was veterinary school.

During summer breaks for three years, I worked on a thoroughbred racehorse ranch for a veterinarian, Dr. Taft. Since my goal was to be an equine veterinarian, this experience would undoubtedly beef up my application to veterinary school. My days of making rounds with Dad and Mom proved invaluable because I immediately felt familiar and comfortable with the routine and process of checking on patients and diagnosing problems. I stood side by side with Dr. Taft when we performed surgeries on these expensive racehorses. I came to realize I was a natural clinician and surgeon.

Although it can be dangerous working around horses, especially untrained one- and two-year-olds, I was able to develop an intimate relationship with these magnificent animals. This connection evolved to the point of being telepathic, which frequently occurs with people who work with horses. The horses were so con-nected to me that they would respond to my behav-ior and thoughts. I would think in my mind, 'Move to the right,' and amazingly enough, they would move. I felt as though I was seeing myself reflected in the horses. If I got uptight, they got uptight. If I relaxed, they relaxed.

I also worked on a research project in the pharmacol-ogy department at UC Davis throughout the school year with genetically epileptic baboons, testing epi-leptic medications. I assisted with the initial studies on the effects of various antiseizure medications. Part of my job was to care for and play with the baboons, which I enjoyed very much. This only solidified my decision to become a veterinarian. At that time, little did I know these would be the drugs I would not only use as a physician to treat my patients, but also the ones I would use to control my seizures after the acci-dent. The Universe works in mysterious ways.

When I was a senior in college, the time had come to apply to veterinary school. My counselor and my parents had other plans. They said, "It's harder to get into veterinary school than medical school. It might take two or three years of trying to get into veterinary school, whereas if you apply to medical school, you'll get in right away." They were right. It was easier.

I decided to apply to both veterinary and medical school at the same time to keep my options open. While I was able to apply to several medical schools around the country, general restrictions in place at that time prevented students from applying to out-of-state veterinary schools. Since UC Davis was the only veterinary school in California in 1982, I was limited to applying only there.

I was accepted first by a number of medical schools, but I was still waiting to hear from UC Davis Veterinary School. When I received my acceptance letter from Northwestern University in Chicago, Illinois, I felt I could not pass up the opportunity to go to such a prestigious school, and their deadline was rapidly approaching. I needed to make a decision regarding my life path right then. I vacillated between the risk of waiting to hear from UC Davis Veterinary School and accepting the sure thing at Northwestern University. With much reluctance, I withdrew my application from UC Davis.

I never felt entirely comfortable about not fulfilling my dream of becoming a veterinarian, but I believed that my parents knew what was best for me. So, I acquiesced and decided to attend medical school instead, letting go of my dream and my passion to be an equine veterinarian.

My first year at medical school was quite difficult. I was missing my family and Jobay, my good buddy back home. I was also looking back at my decision not to pursue veterinary school with some regret. It took until the end of my first year before I could actually let it go and immerse myself fully in medical school.

There were 178 students in my class. It was common knowledge that various medical schools throughout the U.S. had a 5-10% attrition rate. Northwestern wasn't like that. If you were accepted into the class year, they made sure to do everything possible to help you understand your studies and to support you in every way. Therefore, the attrition rate was unusually low. I loved Northwestern, and I still feel it is one of the finest teaching hospitals in the world.

I *fondly* remember the long hours of studying. Our typical day during the first two years was to wake up at 6:00 a.m., dress, eat breakfast, attend class from 7:30 a.m. until 5:30 p.m., eat dinner, study in the library from 7:00 p.m. until midnight, sleep, and start the day all over again. That was my life for two years, nonstop. It was incredibly difficult, but oddly enough, it was also one of the best times of my life. The relationships I developed with my classmates will last forever.

Medical school simply was rote memory, especially the first two years: biochemistry, pharmacology, anatomy, pathology, immunology, and microbiology, to name a few. We all couldn't wait to become third-year medical students, so we could go into the hospital and start our clinical rotations.

We were especially excited to apply what we learned in the first two years to real-life situations with patients. The residents and attending physicians knew we were eager, inexperienced, and still learning; therefore, they kept a very close eye on us. While we thought it would be easier to be on rotations, it was, in fact, even more demanding than the previous two years.

Despite the long hours, I felt competent during the third- and fourth-year medical school clinical rotations because of the rounds I made with Mom and Dad throughout my younger years. Due to this experience, I'd already seen many of the medical conditions about which we were being taught. Evaluating a patient for congestive heart failure, a kidney stone, appendicitis, or a stroke was no problem for me and made learning other disease diagnoses easier.

Initially, I entertained becoming a cardiovascular surgeon because the heart is such a fascinating organ. I found it mesmerizing to watch the heart pumping inside the open chest cavity. The heart is a muscle the size of your fist that transports the life force to every cell in your body. However, life doesn't always happen as we plan, and becoming a cardiovascular surgeon was not my destiny.

When we started our clinical year of medical school, we were each assigned a counselor from the various physicians on staff at Northwestern University. I was given Dr. John Grayhack, the then President of the American Urological Association and author of the book, *Adult and Pediatric Urology*, which, at that time, was considered the Bible of urology. Anything and everything regarding the research and training of medical and surgical treatment of urologic disease was in his book.

After taking courses in urology as a part of my fundamental training, I found urologists to be the most fun and laid-back group to be around when compared to all the other surgeons. I also began to appreciate the wide variety of medical knowledge required of urologists, which was perfect for me so that I wouldn't get bored. Urologists not only had to know about the adrenal glands, kidneys, bladder, and the male and female sex organs, but they also needed to be experts in radiology, general medicine, general surgery, fluid and electrolyte imbalances, and oncology.

They especially needed to understand cancer diagnosis and treatment of other organs because the majority of cancers commonly spread to the kidneys or adrenal glands. However, cancer often presents itself first as a mass in the kidney or adrenal gland. In addition, the treatments for various cancers of the body can have the side effect of damaging the kidneys and bladder.

The urologist evaluates the type and origin of a tumor in order to provide the appropriate referral or treatment plan. Since urologists train in general surgery, they work hand in hand with general surgeons, gynecologists, plastic surgeons, radiologists, oncologists, pediatricians, and internists.

Dr. Grayhack, a gray-haired man with a very deep, stern voice, was a grandfatherly figure to me. I remember my first meeting with him as a third-year medical student. I walked sheepishly into his office to discuss my current progress in medical school and my desire to become a cardiovascular surgeon. I did my best to say confidently, "I'm going to be a cardiac surgeon."

"Oh, they're all stuck up," he quickly replied. "You were born and bred to be a urologist. Your dad is a urologist, all his friends are urologists, and you should be a urologist, too."

Well, that was the end of that. I caved!

PART II

CLEAR THE PATH

Letting go of attachments is the hardest,
yet the most enlightening and rewarding
insight to apply to your life.

Chapter 4

Acceptance: I Have Rights

After a couple of years of living with my parents, I was doing much better. I developed an exceptionally strong relationship with my physicians, Dr. Kowell and Dr. Gerner, and my clinical psychologist, Sherry, since they understood what I was going through and treated me with respect.

Through years of hard work in physical therapy, the muscles of my arm and hand were coming back to a normal size. Only a trained observer would be able to see a difference between my left and right arm and hand. In addition to the painful reflex sympathetic dystrophy (RSD), which I still have to this day, I had a neurological deficit in my left hand and difficulty with fine motor coordination. Despite many tough days, I learned to live without addictive pain medications.

Working with Sherry also helped significantly improve my post-traumatic stress disorder (PTSD) and depression due to the traumatic brain injury (TBI) caused by the electrical injury. I was starting to come out of the depths of my emotional pain, thanks to her compassion, guidance, and understanding.

Sherry is a wonderful person with her own compelling stories. She was the forensic psychologist for one of the first espionage acquittals by jury in the United States (United States v. Smith), which made national headlines. After evaluating the defendant for a week, she told his attorneys that, from the psychological information, it was unlikely their client would betray his country. Therefore, she recommended that they should collect the evidence to support this analysis. Taking her advice, the attorneys did discover substantial proof to support the defendant's position, and after a five-day trial, a federal jury in Alexandria, Virginia, voted to acquit Mr. Smith.

In addition, back in 1980, shortly before Western hostages were held and imprisoned in Iran, she was an American hostage there for over nine hours, not knowing whether or not she would live or die. Fortunately, in Sherry's case, her freedom was negotiated. The wisdom she gained through this experience allowed her to help me even more. Today, Sherry is a professor at a major university and still one of my dearest friends.

Every time I saw her, we'd talk about the struggles I was undergoing. I saw them as problems, but Sherry didn't. She saw them as challenges.

I asked Sherry, "Isn't that the same?"

"No, there's a big difference," she answered. "When you're in the middle of something and feel that your situation is bigger than you are, it's a problem. However, when you find a solution, you now feel empowered to act on your own behalf, look back, and call it a challenge or a life lesson."

"I understand. That *is* a big difference!"

When I recognized this, my perspective changed, and I moved from being a victim of my circumstances to being the victor of my life.

I had trouble letting go of my past and accepting that my life would be different from now on. I was grieving the loss of so many things. Acceptance was, for me, the hardest step. Nevertheless, it had to be done. Since I was living in hell and certainly wasn't going to stay there, I was left with no choice.

I took a hard look at where I was and asked myself, 'Do I want to live in this place for the rest of my life? If I do, I might not make it to next month, next week, or the next day. What relationships will I miss? What business opportunities will never materialize? Will my physical health deteriorate due to the stress I am under?'

I had question after question. Soon it got to the point where there was only one option—acceptance of the fact that I was no longer the person I was before. I hit rock bottom, but rather than staying stuck, I used it as a springboard to launch myself forward.

At first, I couldn't see the light at the end of the tunnel. Instead, not knowing which direction to move, I created my own light. It didn't matter. Any direction was better than staying where I was. I took Sherry's advice and reframed my problems into challenges with solutions. In time, I was able to see the doors of opportunity open. In fact, these doors were always there; however, when I was stuck, I just couldn't see them.

Sherry's wisdom helped me come to terms with the fact that my identity was changing and encouraged me to allow myself to grieve. Since there were so many other people in the world worse off than I was, I often felt I didn't have the right to grieve my loss. When I did, I felt selfish.

Sherry reminded me my loss was important to me and no one else, and I had every right to grieve. No one could tell me how to process my grief any more than I could tell anyone else how to do it. Grieving is intensely personal and unique to each individual.

Sherry said, "Emile, it amazes me that you are not going through the normal grieving process. You're going through all of the steps of grieving except anger, and I don't understand why you're not doing that. Normally, anyone going through your situation would be angered by what has happened to them, but you don't seem angry at all."

I replied, "I don't know what to be mad about. I mean, yeah, I'm sad over my loss, but what am I supposed to be angry about?"

"Well, you're supposed to be angry regarding your injury," Sherry said. "You lost your career, your practice, your identity, and your independence. You don't know what you are going to do with your life. Need I go on?"

"How can I be angry about that? It is what it is," I said. "It's water off a duck's back. There isn't anything I can do about that. That's in the past. All I can do is make the best decisions with the information I have before me, just as I did when I was in the middle of a surgical case facing unexpected blood loss or a complication. My team and I had protocols we followed in order to quickly diagnose and correct the situation. That is what I need to do now in order to move forward with my life."

Sherry acknowledged that my surgical training taught me to detach from traumatic events in order to perform effectively in surgery. Unwittingly, I applied this skill to my own situation and hadn't allowed the anger to hold me back from moving forward; however, she was insistent that I allow myself to grieve.

Sherry told me, "You can't bypass the grief stage. During grieving, it is absolutely essential to be selfish in the sense of taking care of yourself."

She continued, "When we are being selfish in a good way, we are loving ourselves. We tend to love and take care of everyone else's needs; however, we often don't take the time to nurture ourselves. Self-love might mean caring for our bodies through meditation, health and nutrition, exercising, or just having fun!"

I remember telling Sherry that I needed a change of environment for a while. I'd been living with my parents for close to three years, was unable to drive, and had lost my independence. I felt as if I'd been in confinement. At the same time, I didn't feel I deserved to get away because that would be asking for too much.

Sherry said, "Emile, you need some time for you. This is your time to be selfish. Go out and do whatever you feel like doing. Just be safe."

"You know what? I'm going to take myself on a six-week vacation. I'm going to Europe," I replied.

I did just that.

I planned to take a group tour so that I would always be with someone and have a roommate. In addition, I put all the safeguards in place, making sure I had backup plans in case there were any medical setbacks. My doctors approved everything, and I all my ducks were in a row when it came to my healthcare.

I wanted to prove to myself that life wasn't over. I could still do the things I'd always dreamed about even if I needed to take more precautions now. Three years after my accident, this trip was the first time I was out on my own, doing something independent of my parents.

My travels started with a three-week tour of Italy with an Australian-based bus tour company. My 45 trip mates turned out to be a bunch of uninhibited, fun-loving Aussies. They really helped me get out of my shell. Since I'd decided not to tell anyone on this trip about my accident or any of the related issues, I felt tremendously liberated. For the first time since the accident, I could just be myself and be accepted for who I was in that moment without judgment. Rather than shutting myself down, I learned to open up and enjoy connecting with others.

We were enriched by visiting most of the *must see* cities in Italy. In Rome, we experienced the magnificence of St. Peter's Basilica with its incredible dome, the Vatican's unrivaled Sistine Chapel, and the dark, mysterious catacombs. Michelangelo's *David* was the highlight of the Renaissance city of Florence, along with the beautiful architecture of the Basilica di Santa Maria del Fiore, otherwise affectionately known as *the Duomo*. The magical floating city of Venice charmed us with its San Marco Piazza (St. Mark's Square), where the pigeons demanded to be fed and the canals were decorated with gilded, red gondolas. From there, we explored Lake Como, which proved to be my favorite spot in Italy with its lush, picturesque landscape and glass-like lake bordered with beautiful terracotta-roofed villas and their alluring gardens.

I felt as if I'd stepped into history when we visited the medieval town of Assisi, home to St. Francis of Assisi, who is the patron saint of animals. At the Amalfi coast, we spent most of our time in the scenic town of Sorrento, which is known for its fantastic seafood. Their superb dishes quickly became my preferred food in Italy. One of my favorite meals included seafood risotto and steamy, fragrant peppered muscles topped off with the local liqueur, limoncello. Delicious!

Italy provided the perfect backdrop for our lively group to revel in each other's company. We enjoyed lunch at quaint trattorias that epitomized provincial Italian atmosphere and cuisine. The old-world architecture and the people chatting away in their local dialects reminded us just how far away from home we'd ventured.

After Italy, our group went to sunny Greece to see many of the famous remains of antiquity, eat the fresh Mediterranean food, and enjoy interacting with the friendly Greek people. Their open nature only served to enhance our enjoyment of Greece and each other. After seeing the ancient sites, we visited the islands of Mykonos, Delos, Paros, and Santorini. I can tell you that island hopping with a group of gregarious Aussies is about as good as it gets!

Experiencing other countries, cultures, and people on my own forced me out of my comfort zone and rebuilt my confidence. I made friends again after having been isolated for so long and being protective of myself. This trip certainly brought me back to life, knowing I could still enjoy things the way I had before. In fact, my adventures were even more meaningful to me now.

Ultimately, I felt empowered. I found my independence and freedom. I was able to move beyond the need for total dependency, which was a great feeling. This trip expanded my boundaries, making other difficulties in my life become easier. I could now see my troubles as challenges instead of problems.

The interesting thing about having an accident like mine is that many people want to help, and I assure you, I needed their support—but only to a certain point. The more that people helped me, the more dependent I became on their aid. They were doing everything they possibly could to facilitate my recuperation, and their assistance was invaluable.

However, I needed to remember that I was still a strong, independent person with the capacity to move forward with my life. The trip to Europe was key in helping me remember that. I chose to love life. I chose to see a compelling future. I chose to accept the fact that I would need to start over again in order to create a new life and a new identity.

Chapter 5

Acceptance: The Diagnosis

More than four years after my accident, I was starting to make some progress in my life when I got the phone call that turned my world upside-down once more. I'd been living in Philadelphia working as a medical director and consultant for various companies. I happened to be on vacation in Connecticut when my mother called to tell me Dad was admitted to the hospital for a 20-pound weight loss, excessive coughing, and newly found diabetes.

His blood sugar was over 800 mg/dl while normal blood sugar levels are 80–120 mg/dl. During his evaluation, they found a softball-sized mass inside his lung, right next to his heart. His doctors put him on the schedule to have the mass biopsied that day.

Mom said, "Don't worry. It's going to be okay. The doctors think it's tuberculosis (TB)."

"Mom," I said, "that doesn't make sense. The doctors don't biopsy for TB."

Dad smoked two to three packs a day for over 50 years. I knew this was lung cancer. I'd seen it many times throughout my medical career. If it flies like a duck, it's a duck. I don't need to hear it quack.

I called Dr. Damath, the radiologist at the hospital where Dad's procedure was going to be performed. I needed to find out the real story since my parents, trained medical professionals, were clearly in denial.

Dr. Damath told me that my dad developed a large collection of lymph nodes about the size of a softball in the middle of his chest, surrounding the great vessels of his heart and lungs. The most likely diagnosis was small-cell carcinoma of the lung, a highly aggressive form of lung cancer. This would explain Dad's new diagnosis of diabetes. Small-cell carcinoma can secrete a hormone that decreases insulin sensitivity, which would explain Dad's blood glucose level of over 800 mg/dl. In addition, through various x-rays, the physicians found multiple smaller tumors throughout his lungs and a tumor the size of a kidney bean in his brain.

The phone dropped from my hand. I felt weak at the knees and dropped to the ground in tears. My world had just been ripped out from beneath me. My father was my life and my best friend. He was the backbone of our family. Having extensive personal knowledge of this disease did not help because I knew how this cancer behaved.

I didn't want to see him suffer and die from such a horrible disease. Since I knew it would only add to his misery, I didn't want him to go through the dreadfully aggressive treatments for this type of cancer. In fact, I knew that the treatments could be worse than the disease itself. He would require highly toxic chemotherapy and radiation to the brain and the chest.

The problem is that the chemotherapy would wipe out what was left of his immune system, leading to an increased risk of infection. It also would destroy his red blood cells and platelets, causing anemia and increasing the propensity for bleeding from various parts of his body.

However, I was even more concerned that the radiation to his chest would burn his esophagus and trachea, making his remaining time utterly miserable. In the worst-case scenario, severe radiation damage to the esophagus could result in his inability to swallow. Then, the only way he would be able to receive nutrition would be through a feeding tube placed directly into his stomach.

I'd dealt with thousands of cancer patients throughout my career. I'd rarely seen people die from the cancer itself; however, I had seen the majority of them die from the complications of the treatments. Oftentimes, the treatments are far worse than the natural progression of the cancer. Ethically, I wonder whom we are truly treating. Over the years, I have found that neither the patient, the patient's family, nor the doctor want to let go. It is always a difficult decision for everyone involved.

I felt so powerless at the time, just as I did when I was lying on the operating room floor fighting for my life. Here I am, with all the medical experience, knowledge, and wisdom anyone could possibly need, yet I couldn't do anything to save my father's life. Although I knew this was out of my control, I still felt I needed to fight for him in whatever way possible. I didn't want him to be harmed unnecessarily in any way. How was I going to protect him from the very system we both participated in for so many years?

I immediately flew from Connecticut back to Ontario, California, where I rented a car and drove to the hospital. By the time I arrived, the lung biopsy was over. He was in his room and looked fine, lying comfortably in his bed.

Dad said, "Emile, don't worry about it. I'm fine. This isn't cancer. I talked to my pulmonologist buddy, and he thinks it's most likely tuberculosis (TB). You know, I used to work in a TB ward back in the 1950s when I was a surgical resident. We feel it's probably a flare up—a reactivation of TB."

I looked at my dad thinking, 'You've got to be kidding me. Are you seriously in this much denial? There is absolutely no way this is TB.'

Dad's influential personality convinced the medical staff to place him in an infectious disease isolation ward for precautionary reasons. Right about that time, the pulmonologist walked into the room to tell my dad how the procedure had gone. He didn't know I was a physician, and Dad hadn't told him yet.

The doctor kept beating around the bush saying, "Oh, Browning, we did a biopsy of the mass through the trachea and took some cultures. We're going to wait for the pathologist to see if there are any signs of TB. We don't see any obvious signs of cancer, but we might have to bring you back in about four to six weeks from now to biopsy you again."

I immediately stopped the doctor and said, "Wait a minute. You're saying all this crap about TB cultures but nothing about the obvious signs of cancer. Get to the point. Did you get enough tissue to make the diagnosis of cancer or not?"

He kept stalling.

In my disbelief, I demanded, "Don't bullshit us! Give us a *yes* or *no* answer. Did you get enough tissue or not?"

"No, I, I, I didn't get enough tissue for the pathologist to make a diagnosis," the doctor finally revealed.

Incredulously, I asked, "So you do not know if he has cancer or not. Is that correct?"

"No, I don't. I need to go back and do another biopsy," he replied.

"Okay," I said. "Thank you for finally giving us a straight answer. When are you going to do that biopsy?"

He said, "Well, I want to wait about four to six weeks to do the biopsy again."

In astonishment and anger, I replied, "Four to six weeks? He has a softball-sized mass with what appears to be metastases to the peripheral lungs and to his brain. In addition, this tumor is secreting a hormone causing his blood sugar to be over 800 mg/dl, yet Dad never a history of diabetes. Dad normally weighs 170 pounds. He's now down to 150. That's a 20-pound loss in less than two months. The nurses currently have difficulties controlling his blood sugar with insulin, and you're going to wait four to six weeks to get another biopsy to find out if this is cancer or not?

"The way things are progressing, he won't be alive in four to six weeks. This is cancer until proven otherwise. The real question to answer is whether this is a primary lung cancer or if this has spread from another part of his body. Then, we can figure out the appropriate form of treatment. We need to consider his quality of life and determine if chemotherapy or radiation is warranted because surgery is off the table due to the apparent spread of the cancer from the lung to the lymph nodes and brain."

Well, that sent the doctor reeling. "Uh, uh, I, I, I … " was all he could muster.

"Why can't you repeat the biopsy tomorrow?" I asked.

"I'm going out of town, and I think it would be best to let the inflammation from today's biopsy go down. When I get back in town, I can do it," he sheepishly replied.

Sarcastically, I asked, "How long are you going to be out of town?"

"Well, I'm going to Europe for a month," he said, looking mortified.

Even more pissed, I asked, "And you can't refer him to another pulmonologist? Why can't a surgeon or a radiologist biopsy the mass?"

He couldn't answer my questions.

I was furious and immediately fired his ass. After the doctor awkwardly left the room, Dad was mad at me, yelling, "Emile! What the hell are you doing?"

"Dad, this is your life," I said. "He should be repeating the biopsy tomorrow. He screwed up. Period!"

Dad thought about it for a quick second and said, "Son, you're right. That Son of a Bitch! Betty, get my clothes!"

As Dad got dressed, he paused for a minute and laughed.

"Son, let me tell you a joke. Three doctors decided to go duck hunting: a pulmonologist, a radiologist, and a surgeon. They are sitting in a duck blind when suddenly they see a bird quickly approaching. The pulmonologist says, 'Well, based upon its flight pattern and the fact that it's alone, it could be a duck, but it could be a goose or a pheasant.' Because of the pulmonologist's hesitation, the bird flies by and not a shot was taken.

"Soon another bird quickly approaches and the radiologist says, 'Based upon the shadows of the form as it compares to the sun, it could be a duck, but it could also be a goose or a pheasant. I'm just not sure.' Once again, the bird flies by and not a shot was taken.

"Soon after that, another bird approaches and the surgeon jumps up from the blind and quickly shoots it down. He walks over, holds up the bird, and says, 'It's a duck!'"

Dad then decisively exclaimed, "I need a repeat biopsy in order to get enough tissue for a diagnosis. Only a surgeon can reliably do that for me. Let's get the hell out of here!"

I immediately called some of my colleagues (cardiothoracic surgeons and oncologists) at Scripps Memorial Hospital–La Jolla where I used to work in the mid 90s. They got Dad on the schedule for the next day.

Within a few hours of arriving in La Jolla, my surgical colleague performed a biopsy of the softball-sized mass near his heart. The outpatient procedure went well and took less than 60 minutes. Later that night, my buddy, Bruce, a cardiac specialist who arranged the procedure, called me and said, "Emile, are you available to go out and grab a beer?"

I said that I was. Mom and Dad were resting at the hotel.

We sat at the bar talking about life, catching up on all the good times we used to have hanging out together and reminiscing about the surgeries we performed. Then, he said, "Hey man, I've got something for you."

Bruce pulled a piece of paper out of his pocket and slid it across the bar counter towards me. I looked down and saw writing scribbled on the paper, "undifferentiated small-cell carcinoma of the lung".

This was the worst possible type of lung cancer he could have.

I silently paused. When I looked up at Bruce, he said, "I know there is no easy way to break the news to you. We don't see many make it past one year, but your dad is a fighter, so let's kick this cancer's ass."

With almost a sense of relief, I replied, "Bruce, you know I always suspected this diagnosis. I'll tell Dad. He'll want to know right away."

Bruce became thoughtful and said, "Think about it. When we look at all of the patients with aggressive end-stage cancer we've seen over the years, how many actually die from the cancer itself?"

Knowing this was true, I said, "Very few. They always seem to die from the treatments: the surgeries, the chemotherapy, and the radiation therapy. I rarely see them die from the cancer. As physicians, it seems we are treating ourselves, not the patient. We can't seem to accept that we actually have no say in the progression of the disease. Mother Nature determines that. Saving lives? We aren't saving anyone's life from cancer. If we are lucky, we are only delaying the inevitable."

Bruce said, "All the experts gave up on my dad when he had end-stage prostate cancer that failed radiation and chemotherapy. When you treated him, Emile, you got him two extra years without all the side effects. I know you can do the same for your dad."

"Bruce," I said, "I'm not going to let my dad suffer and die from the treatment of this disease. He's going to live a comfortable and productive life."

I went back to the hotel room where my parents were staying.

"Dad, we got the pathology report back. It's undifferentiated small-cell carcinoma."

Dad got quiet. He sat on one side of the bed and looked down at the floor. Then, he said, "Well, six months to a year … "

I replied, "That's what they say, but we're going to make sure we prove them wrong."

He said, "These are the cards God dealt me, so let's make the best of them."

Dad got up from the side of the bed, walked outside, pulled a pack of cigarettes out of his pocket, and lit one up. I was so irate that he even dared to put another one of those cancer sticks in his mouth.

Then, I said to myself, 'What does it really matter? He already has cancer. If that's what he enjoys doing, I might as well let him do it. He's already smoked these things for over 50 years — since the Korean War. Smoking was considered *cool* back then. Taking the cigarettes away from him now is not going to do a bit of good. The damage is already done.'

When we returned home the next day, Dad continued to chain-smoke. About five o'clock in the afternoon, while I was out, he started coughing violently after smoking one of his cigarettes. The area around the biopsy had a scab, and it had broken open. Within minutes, Dad was having problems breathing. My mom immediately drove him to the hospital.

I happened to be at the bookstore when Mom called me on my cell. "Emile, Dad just got readmitted to the hospital. His biopsy site was bleeding, and he could barely breathe."

I knew that, most likely, air and/or blood was filling the space between his lung and chest wall, compressing and collapsing the lung. In that case, if he became unable to expand his lungs to breathe, he would suffocate and die within minutes. I raced over to the hospital and asked the front desk where Browning Allen was located.

"Oh, he's in room 401 on 4 West," the desk attendant said.

I ran up to his room, but when I got there, Dad was gone. I saw his suitcase and some other personal items; however, he wasn't there. I then went over to the nursing station and frantically asked the nurse, "Where's Dr. Browning Allen right now?"

"Oh, he's down in radiology getting a chest x-ray right now," the nurse casually responded.

She seemed annoyed that I even asked the question since I was interrupting her while she was reading a fashion magazine during her break. All of the other nurses on the floor were busy taking care of their patients.

I raced down to the radiology department on the first floor. While I hadn't been on the medical staff at this hospital, most hospitals have the same basic blueprint, so I knew how to work my way through the various departments and corridors. I ran into the radiology department, surveying each area. Since it was after hours, there were no administrative assistants or lab techs around.

As I sprinted down one hallway, an x-ray film hanging up on a view board 20 feet away caught my eye, causing me to stop dead in my tracks. I had never seen the extent of anything like this in my life. The chest x-ray showed the entire left lung collapsed and filled with blood. The heart was rotated 180 degrees and pushed all the way up to the right chest wall, compressing the right lung. The only part of either lung receiving air was the right upper lobe. Without even seeing the name of the patient, I thought, 'Oh my God! That's Dad, and he's dying.'

I grabbed the x-ray off the view board and ran into the hallway looking for him.

Dad was nowhere to be found. I finally located an orderly who informed me that he just took Dr. Allen back to his room.

With the x-ray under my arm, I sprinted up four flights of stairs to get to his room as fast as I could only to find him lying in bed with no oxygen or IV. His face was blue. He was gasping for air and couldn't talk, indicating that he was seconds from going into cardiorespiratory arrest. I ran back out to the nursing station and found the nurse still on break reading her fashion magazine.

I insisted, "Listen to me. I'm a doctor. Call a CODE! My dad is going into cardiac arrest. I need a crash cart and a chest tube."

At first, she looked annoyed at me for interrupting her break once again, but then she realized something serious was going on. I ran to the medical supply room, grabbed a chest tube kit, threw it on the crash cart, and wheeled it into my dad's room. She saw what I was doing but appeared to be contemplating whether to call security or call a CODE.

Finally, she came into the room to see what I was doing, saw the condition my dad was in, and started helping me. Immediately, I placed an oxygen mask on Dad and started prepping his left chest to put in a chest tube, which would relieve the pressure from the blood filling up his chest cavity and collapsing both of his lungs. The nurse popped in an IV and called in other nurses to assist.

Right when I got the chest wall prepped for the chest tube insertion, a surgeon who happened to be on 4 West came into the room. She quickly looked at the x-ray, confirmed everything that I'd seen, and proceeded to place the one-third-inch diameter chest tube into Dad's chest.

Making an incision into the chest wall, she inserted the tube. Immediately, bright red blood gushed from Dad's chest cavity like a fire hose, splattering blood against the surgeon's gown and all over the wall behind her. She connected the tubing up to a water suction apparatus to help draw off the blood. Dad continued to drain over five units of blood over the next few minutes, losing close to half of his total blood volume.

Within seconds, he started to pink up and was able to breathe; however, but now we had another problem. His blood pressure was dropping precipitously due to the immediate release of the blood that was compressing the heart and lungs. Since he didn't have enough blood inside his arteries and veins to keep his blood pressure up, he did not have enough oxygen for his vital organs. We called for O-negative blood to be brought up to his room STAT. In the meantime, the CODE team pumped him full of IV fluids and medications to keep his blood pressure up until the blood arrived.

We were finally able to stabilize Dad without the need to take him to the O.R., and he ended up being fine. Throughout this, my mother was in the hallway, thanking God that I was there to diagnose and initiate treatment since the admitting doctor hadn't even shown up yet. He was still at his office. In addition, the radiologist who'd been on break and hadn't read the x-ray. This represented a serious breakdown in the system.

Although I always knew healthcare had many flaws, this was ridiculous. In less than a week, healthcare professionals made huge mistakes that most likely would have killed my father — twice. If I hadn't been around, they would have. While I understood that the medical staff hadn't done this on purpose, there appeared to be a lack of communication protocols that led to gaps in patient tracking and care.

After this, Dad was in the hospital for another ten days. He kept asking how his little buddy, Roxy, our six-year-old yellow lab, was doing. While Dad was away, Roxy moped around in his absence. We knew Dad would love to see her, so we contacted the CEO of the hospital to get permission to bring Roxy to Dad. Given that Dad worked at this hospital for over 25 years, he and the CEO were close friends. He even knew Roxy and understood that she was a very well-trained, obedient, and intelligent dog. As a result, it wasn't too hard to get his approval.

When we went home to get Roxy, she was lying next to Dad's bed looking sad and bored. Mom said, "Come on, Roxy! We're going to see Dad!"

Her eyes lit up, and she jumped up in excitement. Roxy was barking and running back and forth between the house and the car door as if to tell us to hurry up and get a move on!

On the drive to the hospital, she seemed to know where we were going, although we'd never driven her there before. Once at the hospital, even though she was normally quite calm and obedient, we placed Roxy on a leash. When we got into the elevator, Roxy was sitting there with her tongue hanging out and an enormous smile on her face. Three patients with us on the elevator commented on how obedient and pretty she was. One patient asked Roxy, "Who are you going to see, young lady?"

She responded with a definite, distinctive "Woof!" that indicated the certainty of her mission, which was to see Dad. This was such a human response coming from a dog. The patient said to her, "Well, you are quite the comedienne!" All of us burst out in surprised and amused laughter.

Like a child, Roxy looked intently at the elevator door waiting for it to open. At the fourth floor, when the elevator doors opened, she stepped out, obediently walking on Mom's left side on leash. Roxy caught Dad's scent, put her nose to the ground, and went hunting. She knew Dad was on this floor and was determined to find him. The elevator was at one end of the hall and Dad's room was at the other end, about 60 rooms down. Surprisingly, Roxy pulled the leash right out of Mom's hand. Here was a 55-pound yellow lab running down the hospital hall, stopping at each door to sniff quickly like a search and rescue dog.

About one-third of the way down the hall, Dad's scent got stronger. She bolted down the corridor past the nursing station and made a left turn into his room. Roxy ran right past the doctor visiting with Dad and jumped into his bed to snuggle him. Dad was ecstatic. The doctor was shocked. After a few loving kisses from Roxy, Dad introduced his female visitor. The nurses came in to meet Roxy and happily fussed over her. After that, she was allowed to come see Dad every day he was there. Over the ensuing days, the whole staff looked forward to Roxy's daily visits.

The love and pure joy this beautiful animal brought to us was pivotal. It opened our hearts, and we could laugh. We knew that, no matter what, we were all going to get through this together. We could now accept our situation. Because of Dad's journey, we were beginning to receive some of the incredible gifts in store for us.

Chapter 6

Letting Go: Burn It All

I learned a lot from my dad; however, one of the most valuable lessons I gained from him didn't occur when I was a kid. It happened when I was over 43 years old, in the last couple of years of his life.

By early September 2003, Dad received multiple opinions regarding his treatment for metastatic lung cancer, and he sorted out the best options. The recommended treatment included months of chemotherapy and radiation to the chest and the brain.

Due to his experience as a physician, he knew exactly how horrible it would be to deal with a burned esophagus from the chest radiation. He clearly understood the risks and elected not to have those treatments. Instead, he chose chemotherapy and radiation to the brain, hoping it would slow down the growth of the cancer.

Immediately after Dad received his first round of chemotherapy, his immune system was wiped out, and his white and red blood cell counts plummeted. This required him to be readmitted to the hospital. After a week, Dad recuperated enough to have the radiation treatment to his brain. To prepare him for this, he received the standard high dosages of steroids to decrease the risk of brain swelling caused by the radiation. Dad was sent home with strict orders to take it easy and not overdo it.

For the first few days, Dad was doing great. Then, one afternoon, Mom and I went out for a few hours to run some errands. Upon returning home, we noticed the back door of the house was open. Suddenly, we saw Dad coming out of the house halfway naked, wearing only a grey beret, blue- and white-striped boxer briefs, and brown slippers, pushing a wheelbarrow filled to the brim with household goods. He looked determined as though he was on the mission of his life!

Mom and I looked at each other and thought, 'What on earth is Dad doing?'

We ran to the backyard only to see him dump the wheelbarrow onto a huge pile of items from the house. The pile was about five feet high by eight feet long and contained everything you could imagine: computer software, bank statements, files, family photos, plants, and even furniture—you name it, it was there. If it could be put into the wheelbarrow, it went outside. Moreover, Mom's possessions didn't escape Dad's grasp.

He must have been busy for quite a while. This pile represented at least 20 trips with the wheelbarrow! Mom and I were shocked as we stared at 50-plus years of their memories and possessions. When we looked up from the pile, we saw Dad at the tool shed grabbing a can of gasoline.

Mom screamed, "Browning, what are you doing?"

I ran over to Dad to try to stop him. He yelled, "It doesn't matter! All this crap means nothing! Burn it! Burn it all!"

I wrestled with him to grab the gasoline can, but he had a death grip on it; he was determined to burn it all.

"It doesn't matter!" he kept saying. "Let it all burn!"

Finally, I managed to gain control of the gasoline and hide it in a safe spot.

We put his clothes on and took him straight to the hospital. It turned out he was suffering from steroid psychosis, a temporary side effect of the steroids that came on shortly after his radiation treatment. We didn't recognize the subtle signs until the psychosis was full-blown. Within three days, he was back to normal.

Then, about five weeks later, on Halloween Day 2003, wildfires hit Southern California from Santa Barbara to San Diego. As the burning fire filled the air with smoke and ash, the sky turned red. My parents' house was right in the middle of it.

At that time, I was living on the East Coast and just happened to be visiting my parents for a few days. I was sleeping in my old bedroom when Roxy awakened me at four o'clock in the morning, running down the hallway barking, as I'd never heard her before. She ran back and forth to both sides of the house, but no one was getting up. My bedroom door was closed, so Roxy slammed her body into it as hard as she could, determined to wake me up. It worked. I felt the heat and smelled the smoke.

Less than 2,500 yards away, flames rose 30 or 40 feet high on the ridge next to the house. I could see cars driving down the road as people were evacuating their homes. In a panic, Roxy and I woke everyone up. I grabbed my parents, all their pets, and of course, Roxy, our savior. We jumped into the car to drive to safety. As we were leaving, the fire department was coming up the solitary canyon road to evacuate anyone left in the neighborhood.

The fire department would not allow anyone to return to the neighborhood for five days. We didn't know if our house burned down along with 50-plus years of possessions or not. The fear of the unknown kept all of us on edge.

Not Dad, though. Dad was fully clothed and wasn't psychotic anymore. He was his usual self: calm, sharp as a tack, and more levelheaded than ever before.

He shook his head at the rest of us and said, "It doesn't matter. It doesn't matter if it's all gone or not. It's just stuff. Let it burn. It'll save me having to buy some gasoline!"

I remember looking at him that day and thinking, 'He's right. He was always right. It doesn't matter. Our lives are more important than all the material items accumulated over a half century. We can't take anything with us when we leave this world.'

Sure, on the day Dad had his psychotic episode from the side effects of the steroids, we thought he was crazy for wanting to burn all of the family belongings. However, in reality, we were the ones who were crazy. We were the ones who thought we could hold onto these material possessions, thinking they mattered at all.

After about a week, the fire died down, and we were allowed to return to our house, which miraculously survived the burning inferno. Everything inside was intact but smelled of smoke and was covered in a layer of ashes. Mom and Dad still had all of their things.

When Dad was diagnosed in August 2003, he was given a 50%, one-year survival rate with treatment and only two to four months without treatment. While we were waiting for the fire to end, Dad, Mom, and I discussed his quality of life and decided to stop all treatment. Dad had the faith to let go of fighting the cancer and accept his life as it was. He chose to continue working fulltime as the Medical Director at the Pomona Valley Hospital Regional Kidney Stone Center so that he could be around his friends and keep contributing to society.

Despite living with his diagnosis, Dad was there for one of his buddies, Dr. Getts, a retired physician. Getts was Dad's best friend, with whom he'd shared more than a few scotches during retirement. When Getts had a heart attack and subsequently required bypass surgery, Dad made sure to check in on him.

The day after Gett's surgery, when Dad walked into his room, his buddy was shaking and couldn't recognize his surroundings or people around him, including Dad. Getts was connected to IV tubing, oxygen, and monitors. His wrists were tied to the bed to keep him from pulling out tubes or walking away in his delirious state. Dad knew that Getts was a closet alcoholic. He took one look at his friend and knew that Getts was suffering from alcohol withdrawal.

Dad spoke to Getts' doctors and explained he was suffering from DTs (delirium tremors). "Getts likes to sip on the juice. Just give him some scotch, and he'll be fine."

The doctor wasn't buying it and felt a prescription antipsychotic was the appropriate treatment. Dad disagreed. Later on that night, Dad nonchalantly walked past the nurses' station and snuck into Getts' ICU room with a brown paper bag containing Chivas Regal Scotch under his trench coat. He cleverly buzzed the nurses for a cup and straw. The nurses had no clue what he was up to. Dad then poured his poor pal a shot of scotch, held the straw up to his lips, and helped him drink it.

In about an hour or so, Getts felt *much* better. When the nurse came into the room to make her rounds, she was shocked to see Getts sitting up in bed alert and talking to Dad. They both snickered as they planned their next drinking rendezvous. Later, Dad called to tell me what he'd done.

I couldn't stop laughing. "Dad, you gave him scotch?!"

"Yeah, they never knew what I was doing. I am going to bring him some more tomorrow," Dad replied.

As time went on, Dad's cancer remained stable. However, within two and a half years, delayed side effects from the brain radiation had caused significant damage. As a result of this, during his last couple of months, Dad had accelerated symptoms similar to that of Parkinson's Disease, such as tremors, loss of muscle mass in his arms and legs, and overall weakness.

His physical infirmity became so severe that he required assistance getting ready for the day and settling in at work. Given that his mind was still as sharp as a tack, Dad was able to continue to work two or three days a week up until two weeks before he passed. He wanted to live a full and active life until he couldn't.

Dad's lifelong passion was deep-sea fishing for yellowtail tuna. He loved the challenge of hooking and reeling in *The Big One.* Ever since childhood, Dad brought my brother and me along with him on these exciting adventures.

Two weeks before he passed, my mom, brother, and I planned to kidnap Dad so we could take him on one last fishing trip. We surprised him one morning by rustling him out of bed with no explanation. Dad was so frail at this point that I had to dress him and carry him from his room to the car. My brother opened the car door so I could place him in the seat and buckle him up. We looked at each other and realized that this is exactly what Dad used to do for us when we were toddlers. We were experiencing the cycle of life.

The four of us got into the car, and we executed our kidnapping plan. We drove off towards our destination and refused to tell him where we were going or what we had planned. That seriously pissed him off. Teasingly, he yelled and cursed at us the entire 45 minutes it took to get to the trout-fishing pond.

When we stopped to get the fishing gear at the tackle and bait shop, Dad began to perk up. He was getting the picture. When we arrived at the trout pond, we set him up in a chair with his pole and got him fishing. Since Dad was so weak, we threw the line out for him and helped him reel in the many trout he excitedly caught that morning. Dad was blissfully happy.

It was great to see him in this much joy before he transitioned.

We were blessed to keep Dad around for two and a half years with an excellent quality of life. Dad passed away peacefully in the hospital on April 7, 2006, with all of us at his bedside.

He didn't need to be surrounded by a lifetime of stuff and money. What good would it do him anyway? He needed to be with his family and friends, whom he loved.

We all took our turns saying goodbye. I lost my dearest and most admired friend. I was crying as I kissed him on his forehead and said, "I'll see you soon, Dad. We'll be together again."

As I was inhaling, Dad exhaled one last breath, which went directly into my lungs. I felt it deep down in my soul. It startled me because it was unexpected and synced perfectly with my own inhalation.

While I was saddened deeply by Dad's passing, I knew we'd shared a beautiful life together. He lived his life to the end, knowing what was most important, and it certainly was not his material possessions or status in the community. Having his cherished family and friends around him at the end of his life made him the richest man in the world. I love him for showing me this gift.

Chapter 7

Faith: The Mishap

While Dad's passing taught us to let go, we also learned to have faith in the process of his illness. In the following months, I began reflecting on many of my life experiences, some of which I realized taught me about the importance of faith. I remembered one incident in particular.

After I finished my 13 years of training (college, medical school, general surgery internship, and urology residency), there was a shortage of urologists throughout the country. It was time for me to go out into the world and start a private practice. Some of the most intriguing and challenging cases I encountered during my career as a urologist had to do with pediatric congenital anomalies and trauma. However, there is one case that will always be engraved in my mind.

I'd only been in private practice for two months and was on call one weekend when, at 2:00 a.m. on a Sunday, my beeper went off. I saw an unknown seven-digit number. All I could say to myself at the time was, 'Whatever this is, it has to be bad.'

I immediately called the number, and the Pediatric ICU answered. The nurse asked for my presence immediately. When I arrived, I was directed to an incubator holding a four-hour-old newborn boy with a bloody diaper. The pediatrician performing the circumcision accidentally amputated half of the infant's penis off. Apparently, the instrument used in this procedure had malfunctioned.

Now, this was a serious problem. At this age, the penis was about the diameter of a pencil. What was I going to do? It was now 2:30 a.m., and the nearest pediatric hospital was over three hours away. In addition, since it was a Sunday, this hospital would have difficulty preparing for the case because there were fewer O.R. rooms and specialized staff available.

By the time we would have arranged transport from our hospital to this pediatric hospital, and they would have gotten their O.R. team in place, it would have been too late. By then, the organ would've had no chance of surviving the delicate surgery to reattach it. I needed to make a decision, right then and there, and live with it.

I gave the order to the nurse, "Assemble my O.R. team STAT!"

I asked the nurse to contact the parents so I could discuss the situation and get their permission to operate on their newborn son. The mother was sleeping in the maternity ward. The father was at home asleep with their other children. While we were waiting for the father to arrive at the hospital, I had a discussion with the pediatrician to find out exactly what happened.

"Emile, I've done hundreds of these," he told me. "I don't know what went wrong with the circumcision clamp. I feel just horrible about it. I really need your help."

"Let's not worry about that now," I said. "We have to stay focused on getting the O.R. team together and informing the family of the accident."

At this point, everyone was in a frenzy. The nurses, the pediatrician, and the parents were all extremely distraught. They were viewing this situation as a huge tragedy. I immediately realized that, for the sake of the baby boy, it was up to me to step outside this problem and view it as a challenge instead. When I switched to this perspective, I envisioned a crystal clear outcome. Now it was a matter of implementing my skills, along with those of the O.R. team, to perform this delicate operation.

The father arrived in about 20 minutes, and I met the parents in the mother's room. As you can imagine, the parents were furious and afraid.

I said to them, "While I know you are angry and in shock right now, this is not helping your son. You need to make the best decision for him at this particular moment. Have faith that doing surgery with our team right now is the best choice under these circumstances."

I saw them go through an entire grief cycle in less than five minutes: immense anger with the pediatrician, denial, bargaining, depression, and lastly, acceptance. Finally, they looked calmly at each other and said, "Dr. Allen, we have faith in you. We know you will do your best."

I couldn't panic or dwell on the fact that this boy's life might be altered forever by what the pediatrician had done. I had no control over any of this. If I focused on these thoughts, I would've diminished my ability to go into a creative flow that would allow me to provide the best outcome for their son. My only objective was to ensure that I did the utmost to make the surgery a success. I had to have faith that the combined skills and years of training of my colleagues and me would be sufficient to complete the surgery successfully.

I won't go into the long and tedious four-hour operation, but let me tell you that it was the most difficult operation I have ever done in my entire medical career. Performing extensive cancer surgery was a piece of cake compared to what we did that day. We used sutures finer than the thinnest strand of hair with a surgical microscope in order to reattach the blood vessels and severed urethra.

I created a makeshift catheter from a small pediatric feeding tube and placed it into the urethra and the bladder. This created a bridge so that the baby's urine could drain and the urethra would heal appropriately. At the conclusion of the operation, there appeared to be healthy blood flow to and from the organ, which was a positive sign.

I trained the nurses to care for the infant under these special circumstances. We kept the young champ in the hospital for a week to monitor his progress. Now, only time would tell if this surgery would be a success. We just had to have faith.

After seven days of much anticipation, the *moment of truth* arrived, and it was time to take off the dressing. Was the organ pink and healing, or had the organ died? I slowly peeled away the diaper. The dressing was caked on because the blood dried, hardening the gauze. I poured sterile saline on the dressing to soften it, then slowly and gently unwrapped the dressing from the penis. To my amazement, everything was intact. The blood supply was open and flowing freely, and the tissue was pink. Everything looked excellent! I took out the catheter and discharged the baby boy from the hospital. I saw him a few weeks later, and he continued to do well.

Unexpected events happen in life. Oftentimes, they are no one's fault. A sequence of events can change the course of one's life in a split second. Rather than looking for someone to blame, which is human nature, these parents quickly came to accept the situation and do what was best for their baby boy. If they'd remained angry and upset, their son might not have had the positive outcome that he did. Instead, a delay in taking him immediately to the O.R. might have resulted in another unnecessary tragedy. They had faith that everything would turn out for the best. Thankfully for all, it did.

Chapter 8

Faith: Eaten by the Tiger

In 2007, I was living near Washington, D.C., working as a medical consultant. I still felt as though there was something more for me to do with my life and work. While I learned to accept my accident, losing my dad, who was my rock, was devastating. Mom was also grieving deeply for her husband and best friend, which seemed to accelerate her aging. I felt the foundation of my life was crumbling once again.

With all of this, nine years later I was still struggling with my losses and their impact on my identity. I was emotionally fragile and felt as if I hadn't made any progress at all even though that wasn't true. I was judging myself, as many of us do, and didn't even know it.

A destructive inner voice kept saying, 'You're alone on this earth. You're not good enough. You're a failure, and you'll never be the success you once were.'

That voice played like a broken record. I just couldn't let it go. Since I felt I had no control over my life, I decided that I needed to have an entirely different experience to break this vicious pattern and shift my perspective.

As chance would have it, several of my friends were going to attend a ten-day spiritual retreat in Fiji at about this time. They did their best to convince me it was just what I needed. After much coercing, I decided to go. I felt that if nothing else, flying halfway around the world to an entirely different location and culture would help shake me out of my current state.

When I arrived in Fiji, it was like stepping into a tropical fantasyland. Contrasted by the sparkling, turquoise-blue ocean, the stunning, lush mountainscape looked like something out of *Jurassic Park*. There was abundant wildlife composed of exotic, colorful birds and the local inhabitants, fruit bats, who, unlike other bats, flew mainly in the daytime. It was quite startling at first to see these creatures about the size of a seagull swooping over my head, but they never attack humans and are completely harmless. I gradually became accustomed to these flying dark-brown foxes and even enjoyed observing their activities.

On the way to the ashram (yogic spiritual retreat), the air was perfumed with the aromas of plants and flowers I'd never seen or smelled before. The beauty was intoxicating. It seemed as though I landed on another planet.

Once at the ashram, it was as if I stepped into yet another world inside this exotic island. The tone and presence of the ashram wrapped me in the energy of ancient Indian (India) yogic traditions. The rich aroma of the incense, the vibrant, intense colors of the fabrics, and the calm of this setting immediately transported me to a different space. I had a feeling something profound was going to happen to me.

There were 60 participants seeking inner peace at the ashram. They came from all around the globe and included students, entrepreneurs, professors, doctors, and celebrities. We meditated as a group, sitting in six rows of ten people, three times a day for one to two hours each session. We sat cross-legged, with index fingers touching thumbs, palms up, and a hand on each knee. Our Dasaji, a spiritual teacher from India, faced us in front while he led the meditation for the day. With our eyes closed, he guided us through the chakras (yogic energy centers in the body) via visualization and breathing to lull us into a meditative state.

The purpose of the visualization and breathing techniques was to help quiet the constant chatter of the mind by giving it another focus. Gradually, as I learned to let go of this inner chatter and focus on my breathing, I was able to go into a deeper and quieter place. I found myself tranquil and experiencing true inner peace. Life became clearer with each breath, and I felt free of my emotional pain during that time.

In between meditations, we would break out into small groups for daily teachings. One of the Dasajis, Rajesh, led ten of us through spiritual lessons in which he taught the principles of simple, unencumbered living. I found that these sessions provided me with a new perspective on various life concepts.

After a couple of days, I spoke up and said, "I'm stuck and can't seem to get over this hump in my life. How do I let go of the past in order to live in the present moment or see a compelling future? It seems like the past keeps replaying in my brain and holds me back from moving forward in life."

With a piercing gaze, he looked me straight in the eye and said, "Emile, you need to be eaten by the tiger."

My scientific mind took over, and I said, "Eaten by a tiger? You've got to be out of your mind."

As I argued with him in front of the class, Rajesh calmly stated, "You have to let the tiger eat you in order for you to live."

I just could not figure out what this guy meant. None of us could. I thought he was crazy. I said to myself, 'I'm not going to die and be reborn again literally. I'm not drinking the Kool-Aid.'

For the next several days, I pondered what Rajesh told me and waited for some clarity to emerge.

As we were settling into our meditation time one afternoon towards the end of the week, unbeknownst to me, my patience was about to be rewarded. I was sitting in the third row on the right side of the room. I closed my eyes as I took slow, deep breaths from the diaphragm, concentrating on feeling the air go in and out of each nostril. Soon all of the noise and chatter inside my brain melted away. The silence surrounded me, and I couldn't hear anything anymore. This stillness was similar to the quiet I experienced when I was fighting for my life on the O.R. floor.

Once again, I was greeted by the voice of the amorphous figure:

"I'm not ready for you yet. You have more work to do."

I felt at peace with what I heard, and I wasn't scared. As the stillness engulfed me, my breaths slowed and deepened.

Suddenly, I saw my own body sitting on the ground

while my spirit, as I defined it, was up at the one o'clock position, looking down. I realized I was floating above the room and could see each and every person in all six rows as clear as day. My awareness was so acute that I could even detect the subtle movements of some people readjusting their bodies to get more comfortable. I felt as though I was sitting across the table from them having a conversation all the while observing their facial expressions and breathing patterns. Everything was vivid and clear. I saw our Dasaji meditating with us in the front of the room.

As he came out of his meditation, our Dasaji stood up and told us, "This will be the end of our practices today, and it is time for you to go on about your way and have lunch."

However, I didn't come out of my meditative state. I saw people getting up and walking out of the room. Three of us, two women and me, one right next to me and the other off in the fifth row, stayed in deep meditation.

After some time, one of the ladies leaving the room accidentally bumped me, knocking me out of my meditative state. My spirit came instantly back into my body. I awoke abruptly, feeling cold, clammy, and very lethargic. My whole body and my brain had slowed down. Something told me to take my pulse. My normal heart rate is around 66 beats per minute; it was beating at around 30 beats per minute, and this was after I'd been startled awake. While it felt as if only a few minutes passed, I was surprised to learn we had actually been in meditation for an additional hour!

Gail, the woman who sat next to me, woke up around the same time. We looked at each other and smiled. She had experienced something similar. We didn't need to discuss it; we just knew.

Then, I got up and walked out of the room. Everything was still, and I felt perfectly at peace. I went for a walk down a dirt pathway, noticing the palm trees, beautiful exotic birds, and fruit bats flying around. Although I'd seen these things over the past few days, now it was different.

My perception of time slowed as if I were in a time warp. I felt the animation of the jungle and immersed myself in the movements and conversations of this vibrant universe. The wings of the colorful birds moved in slow motion as they flew across the sky from tree to tree. Rather than seeing the wings moving up and down in flight, I observed the glorious detail of each wing feather moving precisely like the fingers of an expert pianist. I looked up at the palm trees, and instead of the whole tree swaying in unison, I saw the trunk moving in one direction and each of the individual leaves undulating in its own way.

As I stood still in the middle of this amazing splendor, the sounds of the jungle swelled up around me. I became aware of the leaves delicately brushing against each other, the tree trunks creaking and crackling as they moved in the wind, the birds chirping, and the breeze singing. I closed my eyes and heard music more beautiful than any music I had ever heard before. I was surrounded by the orchestra of the jungle.

After this fascinating experience, I went back to my cottage to lie down on the bed for a short nap. When I looked up at the ceiling fan, the blades appeared to be moving in one-second increments even though the fan was on high speed. Now I knew what it truly meant to be *in the zone*.

After resting for a while, I went outside to get a bite to eat. Food never tasted better! I could suddenly detect nuances of flavors I never tasted before in the vegetables and fruits I was eating. I took delight in savoring these new flavors and textures. The peace of mind I attained through meditation heightened my perception of the rest of the world. The sky was bluer and clearer. The birds were more colorful and exotic. The sensation of the ocean breeze was more invigorating and refreshing. Everything was exceptionally vivid and larger than life.

Some of the meditation students mentioned that I looked different and asked if I was okay.

I replied, "I'm just in my own space right now."

They smiled, knowing we were all having our separate experiences.

I finished my lunch and walked around the resort, simply enjoying nature and the peaceful moment. I came around a bend along the walkway and, sure enough, there was Rajesh. Normally, he would have been with the six other Dasajis who gave us our spiritual practices, but he just happened to be by himself, sitting on a wall by the beach.

I approached him and said, "Rajesh, I need to talk to you about something. I just had the most amazing experience while meditating."

After I explained all that happened, he had an especially big smile on his face.

"Emile, you finally let the tiger eat you," he said.

I still didn't quite understand what he meant by that. All I knew was that I felt the peace of another world.

"Emile," he said, "you have been in fear of the tiger for so many years. You climbed a tree to get away from the tiger, but you grabbed a branch and would not let go. You could not climb higher up in the tree because the branches would not support you. You could not go lower since the tiger was below waiting for you. You have been hanging onto that branch for dear life for many, many years. Today, you finally let go of the branch and had faith that God would catch you. You chose to be eaten by the tiger."

I finally got it.

This was the pivotal point in my life. I learned to trust and let go of the proverbial branch, which represented all of my fears and pain that were keeping me frozen. I went from fighting for my life to surrendering my life. No longer was there any reason to hold on to a past that I had no control over. By letting go and surrendering, I was now empowered to open my hands to receive the gifts of opportunity. It became clear to me that fighting for control in my life is disempowering. Whereas, responding, not reacting, to a situation on my terms is empowering. I realized that feeling vulnerable is okay. Surrendering forced me to face my fears in order to find the inner strength to overcome life's adversities.

Being eaten by the tiger is the greatest gift that has ever happened to me.

Chapter 9

Judgment: The Lockdown

As my journey of awareness continued, I recalled another time in my life when I realized how much I'd judged others and how that kept me trapped in a cycle of frustration. About six months after the accident, following a session with my psychologist, Sherry, I remember lying in bed when a new sense of self-awareness crept over me. At that time, I felt ashamed and feared I would be judged for seeing both a psychiatrist and a psychologist to help me process my accident. I even judged myself because of the negative connotation that seeing a therapist represented to me. It was painful.

I found myself reflecting on the experiences I'd had as a third-year medical student in 1984 during a six-week specialty rotation in the psych ward. As part of our training, we were required to take rotations in different medical and surgical specialties so that we would have a comprehensive view of healthcare.

I hated going to the psych unit. I felt as though I was working in a high-security prison because the unit was literally on lockdown. Many of the patients were severely depressed, and some even tried to kill themselves. I didn't understand then why they would attempt such a thing.

I remember one patient in particular, a veteran who had saved lives, as well as taken them while serving his country in Vietnam. Upon his return home, he couldn't cope with society. He struggled to keep a job or friends. For years, he wrestled with bouts of clinical depression and other psychiatric conditions. The final blow occurred when he caught his wife in bed with another man; he snapped.

He beat the man within an inch of his life before retrieving his 9 mm Glock pistol, putting it under his own chin, and pulling the trigger. He wanted to end it all by blowing his brains out, but he missed and instead was only successful at obliterating his face and eyes. After several reconstructive surgeries and years of jail time for the assault, he went into an even deeper clinical depression, requiring the prison to transfer him to the psych ward.

I'll never forget the first time I saw him. The reconstructive surgeries could achieve only so much; unfortunately, none of the surgeries was able to piece his face fully back together. The facial bones were severely disfigured. He didn't have a nose, and the nasal passages were exposed. He was blind because the gunshot wound destroyed the optic nerves to his eyes.

I'd seen some trauma while taking an emergency medicine rotation as a medical student, but this one was difficult to think about, let alone view. Seeing both him and the other patients in the psych ward only solidified the feeling of hopelessness and despair the ward symbolized to me.

I remember sitting in endless psychiatric patient conferences throughout those six weeks, talking about patients in lockdown for bipolar disorders, chronic depression with suicidal thoughts, and paranoid schizophrenia, to name a few. At the time, I didn't want to understand their problems.

My attitude was, 'I'm not going to be a psychiatrist, and I'm not going to be treating psychiatric patients. Just put me back in the O.R. where I can get some real work done. I don't have the time for this. They're all crazy.'

That was in 1984 when I was 24 years old. What a callous viewpoint I had! I honestly thought many of those patients could just get over it, and that, on some level, they'd created these problems for themselves. I didn't have the patience, and I judged them without understanding them.

It wasn't until my accident 14 years later that I would see things differently. What happened to me, and the

long road thereafter, drastically changed my perspective on life and reminded me how anyone's circumstances can change in a split second. The emotional and psychological impact of these traumatic events can be beyond our grasp until we experience it for ourselves.

After the accident, I spent years seeing psychologists, psychiatrists, neurologists, and pain specialists. There was a time when I was so heavily medicated from taking 36 prescription pills a day that I was too weak to crawl out of bed. My energy level was—well, there actually wasn't any. In addition, my weight fluctuated up and down 30 pounds. Of course, I blamed it on the side effects of my medications and everything else I could think of, except me. There were days I remembered thinking, 'If I don't wake up tomorrow, I don't really care.'

It was then that I was reminded of the patients in the psych unit in 1984. I realized I was faced with the same situation that millions of people who are chronically depressed struggle with every day. I used to think they were crazy; however, now I was in a similar boat.

I thought a lot about depression in those days, and I've thought even more about it since. I have come to believe depression is not simply a chemical imbalance in the brain that can be cured or managed by the right cocktail of medications. In my opinion, one of the major reasons for clinical depression is grieving over the loss of something or someone you had or wish you had. When we grieve the loss of something, whether it's a close relationship, our career, our life savings, or the loss of a loved one, grieving can show up as the physical and emotional signs and symptoms that the medical community calls depression.

Research has shown chemical imbalances exist in the brain and body of patients with clinical depression. However, in my view, the diagnosis of depression is often overused and inappropriately applied. So many aspects of physical and mental healthcare are based on treating a symptom here and a symptom there, focusing only on the fragmented pieces instead of helping a person put their life back together. If you ask the right questions, you will frequently find that people are not depressed. Instead, they may be grieving over a loss that needs to be identified and processed.

Problems usually occur when people do not recognize they are grieving and living in a state of numbness. It is natural to deny grief in order to avoid feeling emotional pain. Of course, that doesn't actually work. The pain of the suppressed grief still seeps through like a toxic leak and knocks us out of balance chemically, which can lead to a lifetime of physical and emotional issues.

I know this for a fact because I lived it. I realized I'd been judging myself in the same way I'd judged the psych patients back in 1984. Identifying my losses and letting go of my attachments to them propelled me through the grieving process. My emotional suffering ended.

If there is one message you take away from this book, it is this: your suffering will end when you learn to let go of your attachments and stop judging yourself and others.

PART III

GRATITUDE

The journey to empowerment is through gratitude.

Chapter 10

Gratitude: Living in Appreciation

After I let go of the proverbial branch and let the tiger eat me at the Fiji retreat, I felt liberated. This freedom allowed me to open up to a completely new level of appreciation and gratitude. I began looking for anything to be grateful for in my life and wrote it down. Through this process, I found new significance in a trip I'd taken to Haiti in 1989 during my urology residency program at the University of Iowa.

Every year, Richard Williams, M.D., Chairman of the Urology Department, volunteered one month of medical service in Haiti. In my third year of residency, I was fortunate enough to have Dr. Williams take me with him. He was like a father figure to me in many ways and one of my best friends. Looking back, this trip proved to be another pivotal point in my life although I didn't realize it at the time.

As we deplaned in Port-au-Prince, we were greeted by military police that stood at the end of the mobile airplane staircase with machine guns in hand. I'd never seen anything like this. I was flat out scared. Dr. Williams warned me, "Emile, whatever you do, do not talk about politics, religion, or voodoo."

Our driver, a missionary from the hospital, met us at the airport. We loaded the jeep with our luggage, surgical instruments, and two suitcases full of antibiotics and other prescription medications. To reach the hospital, we had to drive about four hours inland from Port-au-Prince into the mountains. We seemed to travel endlessly over treacherous, potholed dirt roads. I kept thinking about the military police at the airport. They were supposed to be the good guys, so where were the bad guys? I was terrified to find out.

Towards the end of our four-hour trek, we finally started seeing people walking along the shoulder. We thought, 'Man, we've been driving for over four hours and haven't seen a soul. Now all these people are coming out of the mountains.'

We turned another corner and saw that the procession of people seemed to go on forever. They all looked sick, very sick. Some wore bandages on their extremities and torsos. Some were holding onto catheter bags that were hanging out of their clothes while others sported makeshift casts.

I asked the driver, "Why are all these people lined up in the middle of nowhere?"

He said, "They are here to see you."

I was stunned. There were close to 300 people waiting for medical care, from infants to the elderly, with all kinds of medical conditions. They were here to see us because there were no surgeons to take care of them.

As soon as we got there, Dr. Williams and I started working. We saw a woman about to give breech birth, a man with an open fracture of the arm, an elderly woman with uterine cancer, and a baby with a severe abdominal infection from a ruptured appendix, to name a few.

Down the hallway, a man presented with the largest hernia I'd ever seen in my medical career. I said, "My God! His entire small bowel must be inside that hernia." The hernia sack was almost hanging down to his knees.

I looked out of the hospital door where people were lined up waiting to see us. Some were holding old crusted catheters that had been in for months, maybe years, because they couldn't urinate due to prostate obstructions. Many patients had bladder stones, something we rarely see in the United States. There were also children with severe congenital anomalies just barely surviving day by day.

We travelled to Haiti to provide urological services, but that was not what was in store for us. It was incumbent upon us to become primary care physicians, general surgeons, OB/GYNs (obstetricians and gynecologists), ENTs (ear, nose, and throat specialists or otorhinolaryngologists), gastroenterologists, oncologists, endocrinologists, pediatricians, and plastic surgeons. We saw and treated injuries and diseases most U.S. doctors only read about in textbooks.

Since some of the people lived with various chronic medical conditions for so long, we had to perform plastic surgery to reconstruct muscles and other tissues just to make them functional. I was just a third-year urology resident at the time; however, after Dr. Williams showed me how to perform a few surgical or medical cases, I quickly became an expert.

It was customary for the Haitian nurses to pray over a patient prior to an operation. We embraced this philosophy and prayed with them before making our incisions. I operated on patients in one room and Dr. Williams in another. When there was a major case, we'd both operate on the patient together.

As the word got out about the American doctors, 300 people on the first day of our arrival turned into nearly 1000 over the ensuing weeks. There were so many patients to see that we worked 14—sometimes up to 16 hours a day—nonstop. All of them desperately needed our help. My medical training, with the long hours, was put to use immediately.

We did our best to help as many people as we could in the time available; however, we were not just constrained by time. Our limited access to narcotic pain medications and general anesthesia severely curtailed not only the types of cases we could work on, but also the number of patients we could treat. There were certain kinds of surgeries we simply could not perform. Some cases were so far advanced that we didn't have the medical equipment or medications to treat their conditions. Unfortunately, we couldn't help them all. It was extremely difficult to turn people away.

Postoperatively, patients received Tylenol, and that was it. We couldn't use our limited supply of narcotics for this because we needed those drugs for surgery. Amazingly, the patients did not complain and were very cooperative. Their grateful and positive attitude helped them cope well with the pain, knowing they needed to endure this as part of their healing process.

Unlike American patients, they didn't have the luxury of watching TV or taking a sleeping pill while they recovered in their private suite. No, they recovered on army cots lined up in the hallways and rooms of the hospital with barely enough space for the healthcare provider to get from one cot to the next. An open window that invited in the local insects served as air conditioning.

Family members cooked meals outside the hospital on the grass or brought food in from the nearby villages. They brought Dr. Williams and me meals, as well, to thank us for helping not only their family member, but also for coming to Haiti, a forgotten country. To show their appreciation, the Haitians even made us chairs and hats woven from tree bark.

About a week prior to leaving, we got word of a possible coup and ended up having to cut our trip short. We were packed and ready to leave when a man showed up at the hospital in the middle of the night with various traumatic machete injuries. Apparently, a militant group was responsible for this.

While we were evaluating the severity of his wounds and determining the treatment plan, one of the nurses said, "You must leave now! We do not know if the airport will be shut down or not."

Dr. Williams insisted, "We can't leave yet. This man needs our attention."

With that said, we stabilized him, cleaned the wounds, and performed reconstructive surgery. Immediately after completing the surgery, a few hours before dawn, we began the long ride through the pitch-black, mountainous terrain towards Port-au-Prince. Guided only by the headlights of the jeep, we prayed we would arrive safely at the airport and make it back to the States.

As we came around a bend, a group of about 15 men suddenly appeared in the middle of the road. We came upon them so quickly that we couldn't tell if they were a militant group or not. The driver didn't stop to ask and drove straight through them as they threw rocks and sticks, some of which hit the Jeep. Not knowing if gunshots would follow, we all ducked. Within seconds, we made our way around another bend and were out of range. We were so relieved not to have heard a gunshot. With three more hours to drive, we were certainly on edge for the rest of the trip.

The sun was rising when we arrived at the airport unscathed, greeted once again by the military police. Thankfully, the airport was still open. We boarded and flew back to the U.S.

When Dr. Williams and I returned home, once again the dichotomy in healthcare shocked me. The first thing I noticed was all the patient complaints over the most minor items. If they didn't have a sleeping pill, or a second blanket, they complained.

In addition, the amount of wasted medical and surgical supplies stunned me. All of these items were thrown away after one use, or if they accidentally fell on the ground. Of course, this had to be done in order to decrease infection rates. Yet, in Haiti, they badly needed these supplies. The Haitian nurses would've sterilized the items and used them repeatedly until they didn't function any longer. That's how desperate they were for medical supplies, but there was no other choice.

The Haitian people taught me humility and sincere gratitude. From them, I learned the importance of relationships. Materialistic things were of little significance. The Haitian people were remarkably resourceful and patient. Rather than complain, they made it work. Even though their existence was a far cry from our privileged lives in the U.S., their spirits were strong because they empowered themselves within their own environment.

The trip to Haiti proved invaluable to me in so many aspects of my life inside and outside of medicine. I experienced the spirit of the soul to survive and learned the real value of human life, which few people in the

U.S. have a chance to witness. The Haitian people were truly appreciative and grateful. Living in appreciation is living in gratitude. Gratitude is empowerment.

Chapter 11

Gratitude: Answering the Call

At the spiritual retreat I attended in Fiji in 2007, a small group of us volunteered our time to decorate the pediatric ward at the hospital in Savusavu, Fiji. I was the only physician in the group. In all honesty, since this was just after my surreal awakening experience, a hospital was the last place I wanted to spend my time connecting with a higher power. Been there; done that.

From our beautiful resort located on the beach with views of the turquoise ocean and volcanic mountains, 60 of us traveled by bus down a dirt road to the hospital in the poverty-stricken village. Unlike any hospital in the United States, it was a single-story, 15,000-square-foot, cinder-block building. Besides being twice the size, the hospital wasn't much different from the one in Haiti where I'd spent time in 1989.

When we arrived, our group excitedly headed towards the children's ward to help brighten their day. I, however, was the last one off the bus and through the door because I was still in a heightened state of awareness from my magical experience. I lagged behind as I basked in the sunlight and felt the warm breeze on my skin.

Our group was escorted down the hallways of the adult ward as we headed towards the pediatric area. Four out of five of my senses kicked in as my journey down the hallway reminded me of the smell, feel, look, and sound of the hospital in Haiti. Something told me, 'Emile, hold back. Let everyone else go before you. Something is not right here.'

Soon I found myself drawn down another hallway where the group was not going. I saw an elderly man who appeared to be very confused and spoke gibberish lying in a hospital cot surrounded by his family. The man was extremely frail, and by the look of his loose, sallow skin, it seemed as though he lost a lot of weight. It was quite obvious to me this man was dying.

I asked the family what was wrong with him. The grandson said they brought him to the hospital a couple of days ago because he'd become extremely befuddled. The doctor told the family it was the old man's time to pass, and the goal now was to make him comfortable.

I said to the man's grandson, "I'm a physician. Do you mind if I take a look at your grandfather to see if there is some way I can relieve his pain?"

He and his family were very appreciative of my offer.

I asked them to step out for a few minutes and let me have some time alone with their grandfather. I pulled the drape around his bed for privacy so that I could perform a complete examination. Since elaborate blood tests and x-rays certainly were not available at this rural hospital, I had to rely on my intuitive diagnostic skills and common sense. Even though I had not practiced medicine in eight years, my clinical skills kicked in, and thankfully, I was able to diagnose the problem quickly.

Within a few minutes, I discovered that the elderly man was experiencing congestive heart failure from excess fluid in his body. Now the question was, "Why?" When I felt his abdomen, there was a large hard mass from the pubic bone area coursing to two inches above his belly button. This was his bladder. Normally the bladder holds about 350 ml of urine, and a physician cannot feel it upon examination. This man's bladder appeared to have over 3500 ml, or about one gallon, of urine, which is ten times the normal amount.

For a 72-year-old man, there are about ten different possible causes for urinary obstruction. With the limited tools available, I narrowed it down to one. His prostate was five times the normal size and blocked off the bladder. The kidneys, the body's filtering system, were not eliminating the fluids he was taking in or any toxins his body created.

Similar to the way a clogged pipe in your sink will not drain, blockage of the bladder by the prostate causes fluids and toxins to back up and damage the kidneys. When damaged, the kidneys are increasingly unable to process any of these toxins. This results in uremic poisoning, which is an excess of these lethal substances in all of the organs, especially the heart, lungs, liver, and brain. Due to this toxicity, his fluids and electrolytes were also out of balance. Uremic poisoning was causing his confusion, congestive heart failure, and the imminent shut down of all his major organs. He was at death's door.

Now that he was evaluated, there was only one thing left to do — treat him. I walked to the nursing station and asked where the doctor was. I was told he was out in the field, making house calls for the day. He would not be back until 6 p.m., and it was 9 a.m. now. To my surprise, there were only two physicians at Savusavu. One was doing house calls, and the other was on the opposite side of the island attending to governmental administrative duties.

When the doctors were gone, which happened frequently, the nurses took care of the patients. I explained to the nurse what was going on and asked for a catheter. They didn't have one. I found myself thinking, 'How am I going to relieve this man's obstruction without a catheter? A catheter is such a basic item all hospitals should have. In the United States, we throw them away like empty water bottles.'

It's not that the nurse didn't know what a catheter was. She just didn't have one. The last catheter was used on another patient, and new supplies had not yet arrived. The nurse and I rummaged through the supply room figuring out what we could use instead. Finally, we found a pediatric feeding tube similar to the one I used when I operated on the baby boy with the circumcision mishap years earlier. The feeding tube would have to be sufficient.

We employed some very innovative techniques to insert the feeding tube into the bladder while bypassing the obstruction from the prostate. I won't go into details, but it worked. It took several hours for over 3500 ml of urine to drain from his bladder. Although he was still mentally confused, our patient immediately felt better. He was actually able to look up, grab my hand, and thank me as the discomfort melted away.

I returned the next day to see how our patient was doing. He expelled close to six liters of fluids from his body through this tiny pediatric feeding tube. Six liters of excess fluid and toxins are a lot! When people expel excess fluid from their body to this degree, the good fluids and electrolytes leave the body, too, and cause a fluid and electrolyte imbalance. I stayed a few days longer and worked with his doctor and nurses to assist in correcting the imbalances.

The nurses were excellent at helping me manage this severely ill patient. They knew their stuff. Within two days, our patient was walking the hallways and coherently talking with his family. They wanted to bring me to their house for dinner as a thank you for helping save his life. I told them, "No, thank you. Your gratitude is more than enough. You are the ones I need to thank for allowing me the opportunity to help."

It was one of the most gratifying moments of my life as a physician. I was thankful that I had all the necessary skills to help him have more time on this earth.

On the same day I treated the elderly man, the nurses asked if I could help them with another patient. I replied, "Certainly. Where is the patient located?"

The nurse pointed down the hall at a woman who was carrying a baby in a 24- by 24-inch wooden box. She'd just come in from outside after taking the child to get some fresh air. The nurse stopped the woman and asked her if the doctor could look at her child. Of course, she agreed.

The patient appeared to be a two-year-old female with dwarfism and severe spinal deformities. She had pneumonia and gasped for air with each breath. I asked how old this little girl was, and they told me, "She is 22 years old."

"She's 22 years old?" I exclaimed, thinking I misheard the mother due to her thick Fijian accent. "You must mean 22 months!"

It didn't seem possible that this was an adult woman. She couldn't have weighed more than 25 to 30 pounds. I soon learned she was indeed a 22-year-old woman. I was amazed she'd survived this long with these congenital anomalies.

Given that she was weak and having extreme problems breathing, she desperately needed to be on a ventilator; however, the hospital didn't have one. In fact, their remaining oxygen tank was empty, so we couldn't even put an oxygen mask on her. Since there was no air conditioning, it was very hard to breathe inside this hospital. The only ventilation was through open windows, which brought in the flies and gnats. The family used hand fans to keep her cool and swat away the insects. This was not a pleasant place to be, especially for someone fighting for her life. The nurses were doing their best to keep her as comfortable as possible.

I also did what I could for this woman. Unfortunately, I didn't have the specific antibiotics to treat her pneumonia or the proper medical equipment and medications needed to treat her multiple conditions. Sadly, I found out a few days later she died from respiratory failure. Reflecting on her situation, I felt great remorse that I couldn't have done more. I realized we all need to be grateful for our health. It is our greatest asset. A healthy person has many wishes. A sick person has only one: to get better.

My experience in Fiji made me think about the voice I'd heard in the operating room:

"I'm not ready for you yet. You have more work to do."

Immediately upon my return to the United States, I started sharing this experience. I created a strategic plan and mobilized my resources in order to help this small hospital care for their community. The Fiji Medical Mission Project was born out of this. Within six weeks, my resources and I accumulated over $225,000 worth of medical supplies and equipment: antibiotics, intravenous fluids, catheters, wheelchairs, crutches, and other supplies that the hospital needed.

UPS helped transport thousands of pounds of medical supplies to Fiji. I flew back on my own dime to receive the UPS delivery. The shipment was lost in transit for over ten days; nonetheless, I didn't worry. It was out of my control. I had faith the box would be delivered safely. Shortly thereafter, the box showed up in Melbourne, Australia, and arrived a few days later in Savusavu, Fiji.

When the boxes came, the entire staff was ecstatically happy. With the new shipment of medical supplies, the doctors and nurses at the hospital had everything they needed to combat a typhoid fever outbreak that occurred suddenly.

When the mission was accomplished, I found something inside me I didn't know existed. In a time of crisis, when all seemed unattainable, I realized I had the ability to tap into my resources and fulfill the dreams of others.

Helping other human beings without expecting anything in return became my joy. Our mutual desire to give created a cycle of gratitude between the Fijians and me. It was beautiful to experience. This is a memory I will have until the day I die.

When I look back on my time in Fiji, I now realize it was far more than just a vacation or a spiritual retreat.

Since I'd learned to live in a state of gratitude, I desired to give back as much as possible. If I had continued to focus on the negative, which, for me, was being a victim of my accident, I would've headed down the wrong path. Instead, I let go and cleared the path to a new, empowered life.

Chapter 12

Gratitude: My Youngest Teacher

Of course, sometimes letting go is easier in theory than in practice. Life is often harder than we ever expect it to be. I remember one patient of mine, Mattie, a beautiful eight-year-old girl, battling leukemia. She had horrible side effects from the chemotherapy, requiring multiple admissions to the intensive care unit (ICU) during the last few months of her life. The chemotherapy caused her blood counts to drop to dangerously low levels, leaving her vulnerable to various life-threatening infections and bleeding disorders.

Since there was an excessive risk of infection, she had to be in the isolation ward. Anyone who entered her room was required to wear masks, gowns, and gloves, which meant she was unable to feel human touch even from her parents. As she played with her teddy bear and read her butterfly book, her parents, Kelly and Mike, would sit just outside her room and talk to her through the glass wall.

Because of her type of leukemia, she received a particular chemotherapy that damaged her urinary tract. The chemotherapy had chemically burned and stripped away the inside lining of her kidneys, ureters, bladder, and urethra, resulting in profuse bleeding. When the blood mixed with the urine that the kidneys could still produce, blood clots formed.

These clots constantly filled the interior of her kidneys, ureters, and bladder, causing multiple obstructions that made it impossible for her to eliminate the urine from her body. Her bladder was filling up with blood clots and urine in a similar way a clogged drain in a sink fills up when the faucet is left running. Her bladder was practically ready to burst. A urology resident was available 24 hours a day to take care of the blood clots and bleeding in her urinary tract and drain the urine.

Day after day, Mattie cried in excruciating pain. Imagine someone pouring cement into all of the pipes in your house. There is no way to fix the pipes in your home without replacing the entire plumbing system. Mattie was in an analogous situation.

No medications, surgery, or holistic approaches would have helped her at this point. The damage from the chemotherapy was done. Although she was going to die from the leukemia, the side effects from the chemotherapy were slowly killing her and causing her immense suffering. It was only a matter of time before she would pass. Soon kidney failure would occur along with systemic toxicity.

All her doctors and nurses spent days and nights figuring out ways to make her more comfortable. Mattie received platelet and red blood cell transfusions every few days just to keep her alive.

Although she had excellent doctors who worked diligently around the clock to extend her life, I was the only physician Mattie trusted. Perhaps it was because I read to her from *Hope for the Flowers*, by Trina Paulus, her favorite book about a caterpillar's life journey to become a butterfly. Or maybe it was because I snuck her vanilla ice cream from the hospital refrigerator. Even if I weren't on call for that day or evening, I would come into the hospital to take care of her. Mattie was that special to me and touched all of our hearts.

One day, when Mattie was feeling a little better, the oncologist came in to talk to her parents about another round of chemotherapy. He stated it would be a lower dose and not as toxic, perhaps providing Mattie with a little more time. Kelly and Mike immediately came to me and asked for my advice. I told them, "Ultimately, it's your decision. However, if she were my daughter, I would stop the treatments and make her as comfortable as possible. I don't think she could handle another round."

They thanked me.

I prayed they would make the best decision for Mattie. Much to my relief, her parents declined the additional chemotherapy. If they'd chosen more treatments, I knew only more suffering would follow. So did Kelly and Mike. They prepared to lose a child.

Kelly and Mike were angels and handled this difficult time with the utmost dignity. As you can imagine, the identities of both Mattie and her parents changed throughout the process of her disease. Just a year prior, Mattie, who'd never been sick except for the occasional colds and ear infections common to most children, was a beautiful, healthy young girl full of life and vigor. Now Mattie had an aggressive form of leukemia and fought for her life.

Her parents reframed what death meant. As Kelly and Mike saw their daughter become more and more listless and unresponsive, they started to accept the inevitability of her death and began to let go and grieve.

I witnessed her parents struggle at first. However, as they became aware that Mattie's life plan was out of their control, I soon saw them transition to peace. Kelly and Mike accepted the fact that they were losing their daughter's physical body, but not her soul. They let go of the attachment of keeping their daughter around as long as possible. Instead, they realized their desire to prolong Mattie's life was only at the expense of her suffering from this horrible disease and its treatments.

Soon Mattie was in complete kidney failure; her blood count plummeted, and she went into a coma. Kelly and Mike knew there was no further need for the sterile masks, gowns, and gloves. For the first time in weeks, they were able to hold their daughter in their arms and feel her skin against theirs. Precious Mattie passed away a few days later. I was deeply moved witnessing this brave girl's life and death. I was changed.

Mattie was my youngest teacher, providing valuable lessons in compassion and empathy. Her struggles gave me a gift that few people, even doctors, have the opportunity to experience. I learned from her that living a couple of weeks or months longer is not worth the suffering. What I saw Mattie and her parents go through helped me know when chemotherapy and radiation are appropriate or not. This understanding assisted me in extending the lives of many of my cancer patients, as well as my father's, while maintaining an improved quality of life.

Over my career, I was blessed by the gifts I received while caring for adults and children. Mattie's impact on others during her short time on earth was far greater than the intellectual contributions of any world-renowned scholar. There is much to learn from Mattie's bravery and life story.

From my experiences treating thousands of patients, I learned it is not the actual event, such as an accident, a trauma, an argument, or a loss of a loved one that dictates how we will react or respond. Instead, it is the meaning we attach to the event that determines the level of our empowerment. Kelly and Mike understood this. They could have blamed God or the healthcare providers for failing to save their child. If they'd taken that path, their suffering would've been compounded far beyond the natural grieving of their daughter's death.

Instead, they recognized that the medical team did the best they could with the information and science available at the time. They realized her death was part of life's path. Because they chose this viewpoint, Kelly and Mike could go through the normal grieving process. They let go of their guilt for not being able to do more for their child or for doing too much. They were grateful for the eight years Mattie was in their lives. As a result, I saw them clear a path to a new life.

A couple of days after Mattie died, Kelly came to the urology office and gave me Mattie's favorite book about the caterpillar that turned into a butterfly. She included a kind note thanking me for all I'd done for their daughter and them. Kelly even thanked me for bringing them root beer one evening since they considered that a sign of caring. Her gratefulness for this simple act surprised me. I was the one who felt honored for having met Mattie and her family. Her mother was already in a state of gratitude. After more than 20 years, we still stay in touch.

Loss is a part of life. It is normal to question why we lose something or someone precious to us. This is natural. However, that is a poor question, which leads to a poor answer. The better question is, "What else could this mean?"

Now, with a better question, you're going to find a better answer. We can start looking for all the things that are positive, all the lessons to be learned, and all the good that can come out of a tragedy. Mattie's parents did this and became grateful and free.

PART IV

MOMENTS OF

REFLECTION

In every moment, you have the choice to
become aware, accept, let go, have faith, release
judgments, be grateful, and allow the lessons
learned to transform your life.

Chapter 13

Fight, Flight, or Freeze

After all of the insights I'd gained from my experiences, I was on my way to becoming grounded, which meant being my true self, free from emotional pain, judgments, and attachments. I looked at my past from a new perspective and began to identify certain human traits that can get in the way of personal growth.

The fight or flight reaction, a common survival habit in the animal kingdom, affects people, too. However, for people I feel there is one more component that goes beyond just fight or flight. People fight, flight, or freeze. The reason people freeze is fear of the unknown. Paralysis of analysis is the biggest killer of dreams. I've seen companies fail, relationships destroyed, and patients die because they couldn't make a decision. They froze.

There is no chance for a meaningful or successful life when we freeze. I know because I was there and understand what it's like to freeze for many years and see no future. Instead of letting go of the judgments and allowing new doors to open, I used to focus on all the closed doors.

In 2004, I was offered a position as the National Medical Director of ICOS Pharmaceutical, the inventor of Cialis, the erectile dysfunction medication that, in my medical opinion, blew away its competition, Viagra and Levitra. When Cialis was in its final stages of clinical trials, the company gave me a sweet offer anyone would have been grateful to receive. However, four years after my accident, I turned it down because I was still in the freeze mode.

A few months later, Eli Lilly Pharmaceuticals bought Cialis from ICOS. I regretted my decision for years afterwards and wondered what my life would've been like if I hadn't been in the freeze mode back then.

I have come to realize that people fear making mistakes, being embarrassed, or looking stupid. They fear losing their material attachments such as money, homes, cars, and boats. Losing emotional attachments to children, parents, partners, and status at work or in the community also paralyze people. Even though it may not be in our best interest, one reason why we don't let go of the past is that we identify and feel comfortable with it.

Changing and moving into the unknown can be incredibly scary. We are afraid to step out and do something different or new from an empowered perspective. We believe the emotional pain of the change might be worse than the circumstances with which we've learned to live. The state of being frozen is a defense mechanism against moving forward and facing the fear change may bring.

If we are stuck and can't seem to get that dark cloud from over our head, it means we haven't let go of an attachment. The longer we hold onto something that doesn't serve us, the longer we and those around us will continue to suffer. People fear being judged by others as a failure or, worse yet, seeing themselves as failures. We hold onto emotional baggage because we don't want to admit we are wrong. However, letting go allows us to have more clarity to face the inevitable and overcome our fears.

As a physician, I literally have seen people work and worry themselves to death in order to hold on to material objects that were definitely not as valuable as their own lives. Even physicians are not exempt. In fact, many physicians I know have worse health and more stressful lives than the patients they treat. They may even be in denial about their chronic illnesses.

This became clear to me in 2007 when I was giving grand rounds to about 60 doctors at a conference.

Rather than the normal medical lecture heavy with jargon and statistics, I decided to speak from the heart. I felt I needed to appeal to their emotions and their spirits. Since this was not what they were accustomed to at a grand rounds conference, I was worried it wouldn't go well. I wondered if I should give a PowerPoint presentation about the diagnosis and treatment of kidney stones instead. I felt all my old insecurities cropping up, 'I'm no longer a practicing surgeon. I shouldn't even be here. They're going to think this is a waste of their time.'

Fear set in. I was beginning to freeze up. My voice was shaky, and my throat was dry. Sweat beaded up on my forehead. Would I make a fool out of myself? I felt as though they were judging me already.

Then, I realized I was the one judging them even before they had a chance to judge me. By playing small, I was not helping anyone. Instead, I redirected my focus to reaching at least one physician who might be struggling in some aspect of his or her life. My goal now was to reach the audience and assist anyone who might be in the freeze mode.

I gave my presentation with all my heart, showing the vulnerable side most physicians dare not reveal. The audience loved it. A number of colleagues thanked me for sharing my story and told me it deeply touched them. My talk made them think about their life paths and career choices.

I was relieved after the presentation. It went much better than expected. I sat on a bench outside the hospital, looking down as I reflected on the speech. When I looked up, I noticed doctor after doctor walking in and out the front door of the hospital. They all looked like robots with their heads down, shoulders slumped, and faces devoid of expression, which are all classic signs of depression.

They appeared frozen in their lives. I knew this because I'd lived it long before my accident and hadn't even realized it. I recognized they were suffering. I could practically hear the recording playing in the physicians' heads, 'Another frickin' staff meeting. Another five patients to see. I've got 25 hospital medical records to dictate. I'm not going to get home until 8 p.m. and will miss my kid's football game — again.'

I thought, 'Oh my God. This is how I used to live my life.'

About a week later, one of the physicians who'd attended my presentation contacted me to discuss how profoundly my lecture had transformed his life. Prior to the conference, he'd experienced several problems with his practice partner, which triggered a hospital dispute with their contract. In this situation, he was at risk of losing large sums of money and facing an increase in his already overextended workload. He was getting killed. Already on call four to five times a week, he was looking at another increase in his hours without an increase in pay while his partner would work fewer hours for the same amount of money.

He was overwhelmed. It was not physically possible for him to perform under these conditions. Not only was this causing him tremendous stress at work but at home as well. At times, he even felt that life wasn't worth it. He was in the freeze mode and didn't know what to do. After hearing my presentation, he gained insights on how to better address the dispute and let go of attachments. As a result, he chose to let his suffering end.

He changed his focus, took responsibility for his part in the problems, and stopped judging the other parties. No matter what the outcome was, he let go of the need to be right. He was now able to see the problems as challenges; therefore, he only sought solutions to correct the issues amicably. He got all parties to sit down at a table and discuss the difficult topics at hand, which is something he'd been unable to achieve before attending my presentation.

In the end, with his new approach and attitude, the

energy in the room improved. All parties became open to a positive outcome, and the challenge was resolved. I could hear the excitement in his voice as he shared his story with me.

I reflected on how afraid I'd been before giving my presentation to the physicians. I smiled, knowing that changing my mindset and showing my vulnerability actually helped at least one doctor in the room. I'd done my job.

As a physician, my patients frequently went into the freeze mode when given a life-altering diagnosis. Oftentimes, they couldn't make a decision regarding treatment options. Not only were they frightened, but they also had no idea what the near future would hold for them. Looking back, I'd always had the innate ability to guide my patients out of the freeze mode by helping them make decisions that were right for their individual circumstances.

I would advise them, saying, "There are many different treatment options available to you. Please get a second opinion. If you need to get a third opinion or fourth opinion, then do it. Make the best possible decision based on the information provided to you. It doesn't matter whether you have your procedure done with me or another urologist."

While I could always get my patients out of the freeze mode, without even realizing it, I'd gone into the freeze mode myself after my accident. My parents, siblings, friends, and even my doctors all kept emphasizing or validating what a horrible tragedy my accident had been. During the first couple of years, it was very healing for me to have this kind of support and validation. However, after a while, these kinds of comments only supported my stance as a victim of the past and made it difficult for me to move forward.

Some loved ones even said, "What are you going to do with your life? You went through all those years of school. Don't throw it away. Go back to school and get an MBA. Then, you can become the CEO of a hospital."

Blah, blah, blah ...

While it sounded like good advice, it was not for me. Listening kept me in the freeze mode.

In a split second, the 13 years I'd spent training to become a surgeon were gone. What was I supposed to do? Go back to school and become even more specialized and overqualified? Still struggling with my identity, I felt beaten, demoralized, and unappreciated. No one else could tell me what life would be best for me. Only I could figure that out.

This meant I had to push myself out of the freeze mode and take action. I had to look at my life from a new perspective in order to recognize the lessons available from previous events. The wisdom I gained in this process allowed me to reframe the past into a compelling future and create a new version of myself. When I let go of past attachments to outcomes, people, and things, it was possible for me to surrender to an empowered life and be eaten by the tiger.

Don't be fooled. The attachments we carry around are not always of the materialistic kind. They can also be present in our personal and business relationships. It's easy to get rid of the tangible things we don't need. Just get a wheelbarrow and a can of gasoline. However, letting go of relationships can be much harder. These types of attachments can seriously hold us back and keep us frozen.

Consider this: if you listen to people who are judging you, it's going to affect your ability to move forward. Maybe they don't want you to change and create a new identity. They're comfortable with the *old you* they know. Therefore, as you change, they become afraid. When you are evolving your identity, your relationships with others around you are affected, too. They may or may not choose to change with you. Perhaps they will try to place their own agenda on your life, which may not be what you want or what is ultimately best for you. If it doesn't feel right, you need to honor that within yourself and lovingly disregard the opinions of others.

If their negativity is destroying your self-esteem and making it difficult for you to move forward, then you probably don't need them in your life at that particular time. When this happens to you, consider saying, "This is not my life path. I may not know where the road is leading me, but I know I can't sit still. I have to move forward. I hope you will support me in my journey. If you aren't able to do that now, maybe you will in the future."

You are not letting them go out of disrespect, but out of integrity to your true self. Moreover, it doesn't mean they're out of your life forever. You're simply realizing you have a life mission. It just means that, as the relationship stands, it does not serve you in your life at this time. Things may change in the future.

Of all the insights, clearing the path by letting go of people can be the hardest one to achieve. If you are not able to let go, you could be stuck in your pain indefinitely. The choice is yours and yours alone. Don't let guilt, fear of the unknown, or fear of rejection keep you from living your passion.

When you're in the freeze mode, it's vital to remember that it doesn't matter if you do something right or wrong. Just do something. You can correct it later if needed. Going down the wrong path is better than being frozen in place. I went down many wrong paths that cost me financially, emotionally, and at times, even some relationships. That's okay. I learned from those experiences and chose to move forward. My world changed completely when I released self-created deadlines, materialistic things, and relationships that no longer served me.

We all set goals in our lives, but rarely do things turn out as we had planned. That's life! Just move! If you don't, it will cost you even more in the suffering you are experiencing now or may have in the future. Do what feels right to you at that time.

If I find myself upset, in doubt, anxious, or fearful about situations, possessions, or people, I ask myself, 'What am I attached to?'

Check in with yourself and trust your gut. It might be time to let go of an attachment. Go with it.

If something doesn't work, try another angle. If that doesn't work, try something else again. That's what I had to do during my recuperation. I am not saying it was easy. It wasn't. These types of changes are often an ongoing process, and we need to be patient with ourselves. Don't beat yourself up if you're not able to meet your goals as quickly as you would have liked.

You may be in a situation, financially or otherwise, that puts you in jeopardy if you make an immediate change. In spite of that, you can still commit to the decision that is best for you and work steadily towards your goal. The point is that you've shifted from being the victim of your situation to becoming empowered to correct your circumstance, which consequently changes the way you feel about it. This allows you to detach from the emotional pain as you are creating your transition.

Getting out of the freeze mode and letting go of attachments is the hardest, yet the most enlightening and rewarding insight to implement in your life. When you do, you will be empowering yourself beyond your imagination. New doors of opportunity will open up to you like the floodgates to a dam.

Chapter 14

Moments of Reflection

I like to think of this book as a heart-to-heart, as if we've just spent the last few hours getting to know each other over a cup of coffee. Even that is a testament to how far I've come. After my accident, I couldn't even lift a cup by its handle with my injured hand or count change to pay the barista!

I am not a psychiatrist, psychologist, social worker, hospice expert, or life coach. I am a surgeon. I am a surgeon who has seen thousands of patients and counseled their families. I am a surgeon who sustained a life-altering injury and went through the well-known stages of grief, learning to find the gifts in the adversities of life in order to move past being a victim.

I now see that my accident was the greatest gift. It opened up my eyes and freed me from my silent suffering. I am grateful for everything that has happened to me: the accident, the losses, and the pain. Yes, I lost a lot; however, if I could go back and do it all over again, I wouldn't change a thing. If I hadn't experienced these losses, I wouldn't have had the opportunity to realize the insights I've shared with you in this book. It was not enough simply to recognize these lessons. It was necessary for me to determine how to apply them every day in order to improve my life.

All of us would benefit from taking a moment of reflection to seek the wisdom hidden in our challenges. In fact, the situations and people that cause us the most adversity are often our best teachers and offer insights that can make us stronger. Sometimes we don't recognize the lessons available while we are going through difficult circumstances. They can lay dormant for months, or even years, until another event triggers us to reevaluate previous struggles.

While we can't avoid life's problems, we can decide whether we will respond to them in a way that empowers us or react to them as a victim; it is our choice. When we choose to apply our insights to our current circumstance, whether it is a challenge at work, troubles with a significant other, or even a health issue, we will view it from a new perspective. This will empower us to move forward, overcome the challenge, and change it into a gift.

I am not saying that finding your treasure trove of insights will be quick and easy. As a matter of fact, gathering your moments of reflection require a tremendous amount of focus and commitment. It takes emotional strength, courage, and absolute integrity to dive into life's lessons and live your truth.

Life has its ups and downs. I call them seasons. Without the downs of winter, you can't appreciate the ups of spring. Perhaps you are going through a difficult season right now. Maybe you are having a wonderful autumn and winter is on its way. Don't worry. Either way, spring will come. That is the circle of life. Embrace it. Flow with it and wait for a new season.

You may have a moment when you realize that the most difficult events in your life occurred so you could grow and give something back to others in need. I truly believe the bigger the challenges put in your path, the bigger the plan the Universe has in store for you. Perhaps you don't know exactly what you're going to do right now, but you know you have a powerful message to share. The fact that you are still here on Earth means you have more work to do.

Life is a culmination of random events that can become lessons if you recognize the true gifts in them. You don't have to know exactly how the pieces of the puzzle are going to fit together. Simply know that whatever happens in your life, whether good or bad, it is part of the ultimate plan.

In every moment, you have the choice to become aware, accept, let go, have faith, release judgments, be grateful, and allow the lessons learned to transform your life. The process is never over. That is a gift, too, because each day you get a do-over.

Moments of reflection may come when you least expect them. They can float in gently or, at times, shock us into reality. They may bubble to the surface after a significant loss or surprise you during a quiet moment. They may drop in when you're reading a book (like this one) or perhaps when you're frustrated and find yourself thinking, 'Why is this not working? Why does life have to be so difficult? Why?'

Then, something shifts inside, and you have a moment of reflection. All of a sudden, you get a flash of insight regarding the circumstances in your life. You realize all of the experiences that brought you to this point were exactly what you needed. I know, and I hope you know, too, that you wouldn't be reading this book if you weren't on a mission to discover your authentic self. You are now on the path to be *Eaten By The Tiger.*

About the Author

Dr. Allen is a graduate of Northwestern University Medical School in Chicago, IL. He completed his general surgery internship and urology residency at the University of Iowa Hospital and Clinics in Iowa City, IA. He is the former Chairman of Urology and Vice Chairman of Surgery at Scripps Memorial Hospital in La Jolla, CA. Although he no longer uses his surgeon's scalpel, Dr. Allen now heals through his inspirational speaking and writing, touching more lives than he ever could have as a surgeon.

Visit Dr. Allen at EatenByTheTiger.com
or follow his journey at:
Facebook.com/AuthorEmileAllenMD
Twitter.com/EmileAllenMD